The Invitation

True stories
that will
change
your life

ALEJANDRO BULLÓN

Pacific Press® Publishing Association
Nampa, Idaho
Oshawa, Ontario, Canada
www.pacificpress.com

Cover design by Gerald Lee Monks
Cover illustration by Nancy Hamilton Myers
Inside design by Steve Lanto

Unless otherwise noted, Scripture quotations in this book are from
The New King James Version, copyright © 1979, 1980, 1982,
Thomas Nelson, Inc., Publishers.

Library of Congress Cataloging-in-Publication Data

Bullón, Alejandro, 1947-
The invitation : true stories that will change your life /
Alejandro Bullón.
p. cm.
ISBN-13: 978-0-8163-2252-7 (pbk.)
ISBN-10: 0-8163-2252-X (pbk.)
1. Seventh-day Adventist converts—Biography.
2. Spiritual life—Seventh-day Adventists. I. Title.
BX6189.A1B85 2008
286.7092'2—dc22
[B]
2007046604

Additional copies of this book are available by calling toll-free
1-800-765-6955 or by visiting http://www.adventistbookcenter.com.

08 09 10 11 12 • 5 4 3 2 1

Contents

CHAPTER ONE

"Don't Move—Don't Even Breathe!"

That rainy afternoon offered no hint that it would become the most dramatic afternoon of Mauro's life.

A graying fifty-eight-year-old, Mauro was a successful business executive. His parents had immigrated to the country where he now lived when he was just a boy. During the first years in their new homeland, the family had endured times of poverty. That was then. Things had changed. Life had been good to Mauro. He had progressed from street vendor to owner of a chain of lucrative clothing stores. He was a rich man who enjoyed his life.

When Mauro drove out of the parking lot late that afternoon, the sky was darkening, and the traffic was dense, as it is in any big city at the end of the workday when people are heading home. He drove the same route that he always did. He was tired. What he wanted most was to get into his shower at home and feel the water kneading his body.

What happened next occurred with amazing speed. A black Jeep Cherokee turned in front of Mauro. To avoid a collision, he hit his brakes and swerved to the side of the road.

Immediately, a dark pickup pulled in behind him, blocking him in. Three armed men jumped out of the pickup, grabbed him out of his car, and forced him into the backseat of the Cherokee. Then someone put a hood over his head, pushed him to the floor, and pressed the barrel of a revolver into his neck.

Mauro couldn't understand what was happening. "What do you want? Where are you taking me?" he asked.

A deep voice replied, "If you cooperate, we won't hurt you. Now shut up, and don't move—don't even breathe!"

Mauro had heard stories of kidnappings. Someone had even suggested that he shouldn't follow the same route on his commute every day and that he should hire security guards to accompany him. But it all seemed unnecessary. He never thought he would be a victim of the violence that spreads like a plague in big urban centers. Now, fear clutched his heart.

When the kidnappers reached their mysterious destination, they walked him inside, tied his hands, and shut him up in a dark place. There were no threats, no explanations—only a cruel silence. Silence is the most effective weapon criminals can use to dominate their prey psychologically and transform them into submissive, obedient victims.

Hours passed. Mauro could hear the kidnappers celebrating their success. He wept silently. Though he hadn't been a religious person, he also begged for divine mercy and asked for help.

He told the kidnappers he needed to go to the bathroom. No one paid any attention. Eventually, out of sheer exhaustion, he fell asleep in urine-soiled pants—terrified, with no idea where he was or what his kidnappers wanted.

When Mauro awoke, the hood still covered his head, and he was finding it hard to breathe. He got up and began to stumble blindly around his prison. Apparently, he was in a cubicle ten feet square. He felt as though he would go crazy wondering what his kidnappers were planning. He wished they would talk—then maybe he could make sense of the whirlwind of thoughts that spun in his mind.

Several hours after Mauro awoke, the criminals allowed him to take a bath, change his clothes, and eat a piece of cold pizza. They took him into a room where there was a bed and a mattress. Then a masked man with a deep voice and a revolver in his fist, spoke in the slang of the underworld. "Nothing will happen to you as long as you and your family cooperate," he said. "We'll feed you and let you go to the bathroom, but we'll be watching. Don't try to escape. It's all over if you do something stupid like that. You're completely in our control. The best thing you can do to help yourself is to help us so that we can end this as soon as possible."

For the next week, no one said a word to Mauro. At the end of the week, they told him to write a note to his family asking them to pay the ransom. Then they took a picture of him holding up that day's newspaper and stopped talking to him again.

As long weeks passed, Mauro lost all notion of time. Anguish, despair, bitterness, hate, the desire to kill—feelings he had never before known—now filled the hours. These criminals acted as though they owned the world. To them, Mauro was nothing more than an object—a bag of potatoes. A bag of potatoes to be sold for two million dollars. That is what the kidnappers were demanding. But Mauro's family couldn't collect that much money.

The delay angered the kidnappers. One day they came in, furious, yelling and shouting. They struck Mauro on the head, knocking him unconscious. When he woke up, his left ear hurt terribly, and he could feel something wet—blood—running down his neck. He raised his hand to his head and found that the kidnappers had cut off a piece of his ear. They sent it to his family to prove they were serious about their demands.

Their crude message brought results. Within forty-eight hours, the family paid half a million dollars, and the kidnappers abandoned Mauro in a suburb of the city. They had held him captive for two months.

*   *   *   *   *

Most people who had survived a brutal kidnapping would thank God, hug their loved ones, and try to forget the past. Mauro reacted differently. He seemed to have lost all interest in life. He didn't return to work. Instead, he lived like a zombie, shutting himself in his room for hours. When people spoke to him, he said little, and as often as not, what he did say stung.

Mauro even brushed aside the love of his family and friends. No one could penetrate the silent world of his thoughts, not even his beloved ten-year-old grandson. "What are you thinking about, Grandpa?" the boy would ask. "Nothing, sonny," Mauro would reply. Then, hugging the only human being who could touch his numb feelings, he would cry.

Lying in the darkness of his room with his eyes wide open, Mauro would look toward the ceiling as if trying to draw on it an image of the only face he had seen during the eight weeks of his captivity. It was a round face and too young for the prominent baldness that exposed a scar about two inches long on the man's scalp.

Mauro wanted to forget what had happened. The memories were destroying him. But at the same time, he held on to those memories. He thought that if he could eliminate that man, he would be free from the prison that held him captive. His desire for self-administered "justice"—for vengeance—grew stronger every day.

Eventually, Mauro began returning to work and to his previous routine. By the time he had been home for three months, his life had returned to normal—except for one thing. He would disappear for hours. Nobody knew where he went. He hadn't been secretive before the kidnapping. Now he seemed to be hiding something. His family thought maybe he was having an affair.

Mauro's family was wrong. He was roaming the city. He was taking the bus, the train, the metro and moving from place to place. And he was watching people. Staring at them. He was looking for something. For someone.

One hot, bright afternoon Mauro stood in the doorway of a bar, drinking a bottle of water and watching the passersby. Suddenly, his heart beat faster, and he almost dropped the water bottle. It was him! Without any doubt, that was the face. Mauro would never forget it, no matter how long he lived.

He'd spent two years searching. Finding the only kidnapper he could have recognized was like finding a needle in a haystack. He wanted to shout, to call the police, to tell the whole world that this apparently harmless man was a dangerous kidnapper. He felt a mixture of terror and hate. He wanted to pounce on the man, but he was cold-blooded enough to control himself.

Keeping a discreet distance, Mauro trailed the man. The kidnapper walked to a train station and took a train to the suburbs, where he boarded a bus. He never noticed that he was being followed. When he got off the bus, he walked a little way and then entered a yellow, two-story house. Some children were playing soccer in a nearby vacant lot. Mauro sat down as if to watch the game, but he kept an eye on the house. When a girl who looked to be about ten years old sat down beside him, he questioned her about the man.

As night approached, Mauro took a bus downtown and then hailed a taxi. During his ride home, a strange sense of relief washed through him—and a happiness that he hadn't felt in the past two years. He knew exactly what he would do now. He'd been planning ever since the kidnapping.

Not long after Mauro found the kidnapper, he went to a large park in the city and sat on a particular bench. The man who had specified the bench came at exactly 6:00 P.M. "Call me Negão," he said. He was tall, strong, and taciturn, and he belonged to an assassination squad. They would do any kind of dirty job for a price. They would locate and kill all the people involved in Mauro's kidnapping. Mauro was to pay half the agreed price the following day and the other half when he saw the corpses.

Anyone who had known Mauro before the kidnapping would have found it hard to believe that he, an exemplary father, faithful husband, and good friend, could have planned such a horrendous act. But then all of us are surprised by the attitudes we see in other people, to say nothing of those we find in ourselves. We forget that a beast lurks inside each of us—a beast that is capable of the worst actions.

All of us are born with a sinful nature—an innate tendency toward evil. Culture, education, and self-discipline may tame our words and actions, but no human effort can ever change what lies inside. The beast crouches in the hidden world of thoughts and feelings, ready to attack at the very first slip. The prophet Jeremiah said,

> "The heart is deceitful above all things,
> And desperately wicked;
> Who can know it?" (Jeremiah 17:9).

And the apostle Paul wrote, " 'There is none righteous, no, not one. . . . There is none who does good, no, not one' " (Romans 3:10, 12). He expressed the despair of those who realize the futility of their efforts to control that beast: "O wretched man that I am! Who will deliver me from this body of death?" (Romans 7:24).

Mauro was living this painful truth even though he wasn't conscious of it. Until the moment of the kidnapping, that beast had been hidden inside his heart, waiting for an opportune moment to attack. Now the time had come. All the pain and humiliation he had suffered at the hands of the criminals had awakened the beast within him, making him capable of planning a barbarous crime.

*   *   *   *   *

At 3:00 A.M. on a hot summer night, Mauro's cell phone vibrated. He got up silently and went into the living room to answer the call.

"You have one hour to get here," Negão informed him. "We have the six 'packages,' and we need to get rid of them before sunrise."

The rendezvous was forty-three miles away, across the city and down a narrow, one-way road, the last six and a half miles of which were unpaved, rocky, and winding. Mauro drove there in less than fifty minutes, running every red light on his route.

Eventually, Mauro saw the lights of a car that was waiting beside the road. The lights blinked on and off—the signal he was looking for. Trembling and sweating, he parked his car.

Four men were standing in a clearing near the road. Negão, one of the four, was the only one who spoke. "There they are; take a good look," he said. "The first one squealed." The killing squad had tortured the man Mauro had found till he revealed the identity and whereabouts of the others.

The six corpses were lying in a row on the ground. Negão shone a flashlight on their faces, and Mauro looked at them one by one. Suddenly his heart skipped a beat. "Wait! Wait!" he yelled. Grabbing the flashlight, he shone it again on the face of the fourth corpse. It seemed to him that the earth shook under his feet, and he nearly screamed in pain. "No way!" he shouted. "You guys have made a mistake—a terrible mistake! That man is my best friend. He couldn't have been involved!"

For the first time, Negão's voice seemed almost human. "We didn't make any mistakes," he said softly. "I know it must seem hard, but your 'best friend' is the one who paid the gang and got the better part of the ransom."

Mauro felt like vomiting. He began sobbing uncontrollably. Then he circled the corpse of his friend shouting, "No way, you wretch! You couldn't have done this to me!"

Eventually, the assassins told him, "Get out of here, or you're going to get into trouble." Mauro got into his car, put the pedal to the floor, and flew down the road as if he wanted to die. He drove around aimlessly until the car ran out of gas and rolled to a stop. The police found him stopped on the highway, head on the steering wheel, asleep. When they woke him up, he was incoherent. They could identify him only by the documents he had in his pocket. It was apparent that he was suffering from some kind of mental breakdown.

Mauro kept insisting that the police must arrest him. "I'm a murderer!" he shouted. "I just killed my best friend, and I deserve to die!" But when the police interrogated him, he could give no information about the supposed crime. He could only cry and beat his head on the wall.

Late that night, the police called Mauro's family. His oldest sons hurried to the police station and brought him home.

* * * * *

Mauro's condition continued to decline. He went for days without sleeping. He would go into the garden at night and pace continually around the swimming pool, sometimes howling like a wolf.

The family took him to the best specialists. None of them could explain what had become of him. To help him sleep, they gave him powerful tranquilizers. But nothing seemed to work. At times, he became an aggressive, dangerous person. At other times, he was apathetic and indifferent. Occasionally, he acted catatonic, refusing to eat and staring for hours at some invisible point on the horizon.

Ten painful years passed. Mauro spent much of that time as a patient in various clinics for the mentally ill. During the last few months of the eleventh year, he seemed a bit improved. The doctors thought that a few days spent with his family would be good for him. They were wrong. Taking advantage of a moment when he wasn't being watched, Mauro swallowed a whole bottle of tranquilizers. His wife discovered what he'd done and rushed him to the nearest hospital in time to save his life. This was the third time he had attempted suicide since his kidnapping.

That Christmas season was the saddest the family had ever experienced. The comfortable life that their beloved husband and father had provided through years of hard work didn't mitigate the terrible pain of seeing him in such anguish. What had happened that mysterious morning when he had left the house so early? Where had he gone? What could have caused such a complete mental collapse? Everyone tried to find the connection between his sudden disappearances after the kidnapping and the dramatic experience they were living now. No one could figure it out.

The family knew of a retreat for people suffering from depression run by the Seventh-day Adventist Church. It was located on the side of a majestic mountain. It had excellent recommendations; business leaders, movie stars, and other famous people had found peace and recovery there. Previously, Mauro's family had dismissed the idea of taking him there because of their bias against religion. But the terrible impact of the latest suicide attempt made them willing to try just about anything that offered hope. So they took Mauro to the clinic.

The clinicians gradually decreased the dosage of the medications he was taking, sending him instead on long daily walks and feeding him a diet consisting of fruits, grains, and vegetables. They also provided a spiritual counselor. This man noticed that Mauro spent most of his time in his room. He didn't participate in any group activities other than those that were required as part of his treatment. Lost in thought, he would weep silently. The counselor found it very difficult to talk with him. His answers were cursory, and he made it evident that he didn't want to converse with anyone.

One day the counselor approached Mauro as he was resting in the shade of a flame tree. "You needn't talk," he said in a friendly voice, "just listen to me. I'm going to tell you a story. If you don't like the story, just tell me, and I'll stop bothering you."

Mauro shrugged his shoulders indifferently, so the counselor proceeded to tell Mauro the following story:

> Once upon a time there was a man who was king of a powerful nation. One day while his army was away at war, this king went up on the roof of his palace. As he

scanned the city below him, he saw the wife of one of his best generals taking a bath.

Desire for this beautiful woman filled the king's heart. At first, he resisted his feelings. But instead of squelching them, he fantasized about the woman until his lust became uncontrollable. Since he was king, he could do as he pleased, and she gave in, so they both sinned.

When the king was alone again, he felt as though a huge weight were crushing him. He couldn't sleep. He wept because he knew his behavior was evil, and the memory of it tormented him. *But,* he thought, *at least no one saw us. Soon it will all be forgotten.*

However, some weeks later, the woman told him that she was pregnant. "And I don't have any explanation to give," she said. "My husband is away at war, and it's obvious he couldn't be the child's father."

The king nearly went crazy. What would he tell his people? Why had he gotten involved with the wife of a general who was fighting his war? His image would be tarnished, and his kingdom would be at risk. No, the people must never know what happened.

For days the king pondered one plan after another, trying to think of some way to cover up his sin. Then, in desperation, he did something he never would have imagined he could do. He ordered one of his trusted chief officers to arrange an "accident" so that the inconvenient general would be killed in battle. It was done. Then, in apparent kindness, the king married the widow, saying that the least he could do for the general who was slain while fighting for him was to take care of his wife.

From that day on, the king tried to forget the crime he had committed. He constantly told himself that nothing had happened. He tried to justify himself—to explain and rationalize his sin. Nothing worked. His sin was always there, tormenting him night and day.

The Bible says,

> "Though you wash yourself with lye, and use
>   much soap,
> Yet your iniquity is marked before Me, says the
>   Lord God" [Jeremiah 2:22].

And wise King Solomon wrote,

> He who covers his sins will not prosper,
> But whoever confesses and forsakes them will
>   have mercy [Proverbs 28:13].

There is only one way people can rid themselves of their sins. They must repent, confess them, and abandon them. But the king continued to try to hide his sin.

Then one day, a prophet appeared in the royal court. "King," he said, "please help me. I have a case I don't know how to handle."

The king said, "What's the matter?"

"In one of our cities," said the prophet, "lives a rich man who has many sheep and a poor man who had only one little lamb, which he raised just like a member of his family. One day, a visitor came to the rich man's house, and the rich man slaughtered the poor man's only lamb to make a feast for his friend. What should we do with this rich man?"

The king's face turned red with anger. In great indignation he declared, "That wretch must die!"

The prophet waited for a moment. Then he looked at the king with love and said, "My king, you are that man. You had your choice of all the women in the kingdom, but you took your general's only wife."

The king felt naked. The shame of his sin was exposed. He fled from the presence of the prophet and cried into the silence of the night, "I'm a murderer! I deserve to die! My hands are stained with blood."

He ran into a cave, where he knelt and cried out,
Have mercy upon me, O God,
According to Your lovingkindness;
According to the multitude of Your tender mercies,
Blot out my transgressions. . . .

For I acknowledge my transgressions,
And my sin is always before me.
Against You, You only, have I sinned,
And done this evil in Your sight [Psalm 51:1, 3, 4].

We don't know how long the king was in that cave. However, when he came out, there was peace in his heart. He was a new man. He had been forgiven. A new day dawned for him, and he went back to the palace ready to enjoy life with the people he loved.

When the counselor finished the story, Mauro was staring into space and tears were streaming down his cheeks. The counselor put a hand on his shoulder and waited until he calmed down. Then he read him a promise from the Bible: " 'If we confess our sins, He is faithful and just to forgive us our sins and to cleanse us from all unrighteousness' " (1 John 1:9).

The counselor knew that he had touched a sore spot. Guilt was destroying Mauro. It is fully capable of doing that. It's like an executioner who crucifies people every day on the cross of their own conscience. Many people tormented by guilt give up on themselves, sometimes even ending their lives in suicide.

From that day on, whenever Mauro saw that the counselor was alone, he would—without saying a word—walk over and sit down beside him. Then the counselor would read to him biblical promises about forgiveness, such as,

> "Come now, and let us reason together,"
> Says the LORD,
> "Though your sins are like scarlet,
> They shall be as white as snow;
> Though they are red like crimson,
> They shall be as wool" (Isaiah 1:18).

One day the counselor offered to pray for Mauro. When Mauro acquiesced, he placed a hand on his shoulder and said, "Lord, this man is Your son. He needs Your mercy and Your forgiveness. I don't know his past, but I know that guilt is destroying him. Please, Lord, be merciful and forgive his sins—"

Sobbing loudly, Mauro interrupted the counselor's prayer. "I'm a murderer!" he said. "Oh my God, I'm a murderer. I don't deserve to live. Take my life! I want to end this hell of a life."

The counselor put his arm around Mauro's shoulders and whispered in his ear, "You don't need to die. Jesus already paid the price of your sins with His death."

"That can't be!" Mauro protested. "You're saying that only because you don't know what I did. If you knew, you would know my sin can't be forgiven."

To that the counselor replied by reading Jesus' own words: " ' "I say to you, every sin . . . will be forgiven men" ' " (Matthew 12:31). "Do you understand what that means?" he asked Mauro. " 'Every sin' means *every sin:* murder, robbery, prostitution, homosexual practices—the worst of the worst. Divine forgiveness has no limit."

Mauro began to cry. He hugged the counselor as tightly as if he were his only link to salvation. "Please don't leave me," he begged. "Don't abandon me."

For years and years this man had been shut up in the dark prison of guilt, loneliness, and self-condemnation. Ever since that dreadful night, he had wished to die. He thought death was the only way out of his suffering. Now, a sliver of light had broken into his dark world of fear and guilt.

Mauro's recovery was rapid. The next time his family came to visit, he smiled at them. It was the first time that he had done so in many years. True, he smiled timidly, as if they were strangers, but he looked into their eyes. And he seemed to be at peace. They couldn't understand what was happening. Only the counselor and Mauro knew.

Mauro spent hours studying the Bible with the counselor. He read the prophet Isaiah's words:

> Your iniquities have separated you from your God;
> And your sins have hidden His face from you (Isaiah
>   59:2).

Then he understood why he'd had no peace. He'd been separated from Jesus, the only One who could give him peace. Now, however, he believed Jesus' promise: " 'Peace I leave with you, My peace I give to you' " (John 14:27).

Mauro also learned that divine forgiveness means more than

just liberation from guilt. It isn't just a statement of acquittal. The Bible clearly says both that "the wages of sin is death" and that "all have sinned and fall short of the glory of God" (Romans 6:23; 3:23). In other words, death always follows sin. All human beings are sinners, so we all should have died—then justice would have been served.

> But He was wounded for our transgressions,
> He was bruised for our iniquities;
> The chastisement for our peace was upon Him,
> And by His stripes we are healed (Isaiah 53:5).

What Person was Isaiah talking about? Who suffered on our behalf? Mauro learned that Jesus is the central Person in the gospel. " 'Nor is there salvation in any other, for there is no other name under heaven given among men by which we must be saved' " (Acts 4:12).

Mauro's mind had been like a dark room in which threatening creatures tormented him constantly. Suddenly, through a crack in his conscience, a sunbeam had shone in. The liberating gospel of Christ had flooded his being with peace and happiness.

*   *   *   *   *

The digital clock on the dashboard showed the time: 3:00 A.M. We still had four hours of driving ahead of us. While our car devoured the miles from Rio de Janeiro to Bahia that early morning, my companion, visibly moved, told me Mauro's story. He was the man God had used to bring the gospel of forgiveness to Mauro's tormented mind. He was the chaplain.

24

CHAPTER TWO

"Mommy, Don't Leave Me!"

The neon lights blinked on and off, announcing the name of the nightclub: Extasy. But Lilian's life was far from ecstatic. She was cold, hungry, tired, fearful, and depressed.

Lilian was afraid to enter the nightclub. She knew that if she did, she would be starting down a path from which there was no turning back. She feared that she would be destroying the values she cherished, even though she often questioned the point of holding those values in such a cruel world.

But what else could she do? Life had brought her to this crossroad. And in a way, going in might punish God for the hard life He'd given her ever since she was a defenseless little girl.

She went in. The odor inside was nauseating. It was the stench of false promises, of forbidden things, of sin. Her body and her heart trembled. She wanted to get out of there, to run away. But run away to where? Back to the life of scarcity and poverty she was living? *Sometimes one must choose things one doesn't really want. I have no other choice. I need to survive.* At least that is what she kept telling herself.

She waited at an empty table for the friend who had promised to introduce her to the owner of the nightclub. Pleasure-hungry men were devouring the girls dancing on the stage with their eyes. The deafening music kept her from thinking. It was better that way. To survive in a place like this, she would have to be anesthetized.

Who am I, and what am I doing here? she asked herself. Her mind drifted to the past, to the years of her childhood in the country. Her first memory was of herself at four years old crying, "Mommy, don't leave me!" beside the corpse of her mother.

The first time she had said those words audibly, her mother could no longer hear them. She had repeated that cry inaudibly many times since, in hours of loneliness, sadness, and difficulty. But no one ever heard her. Not when she was hungry. Not when she was cold. Not even when her stepfather raped her when she was ten years old.

She had spent her adolescence with a poor family. She had finished high school and the first year of college in a school of architecture. Then she had run out of money. She'd spent the next two years searching for a way to survive and continue her education, but she hadn't found a job that would allow her to fulfill her dream of becoming an architect. The little money she earned was barely enough to pay for room and board. Now she was living in a city with more than two million inhabitants, and as always, she was alone.

Then she met Tina.

"You don't need to live this way," Tina had told her. "You're young and pretty. There are many men who would give their life for you."

Tina knew nothing of dreams. Maybe she had never had them. Maybe she had lost them in the sea of difficulties one has to cross to reach them. She seemed to be a consumer; the only thing that mattered to her was money. Apparently, she had plenty of it—she dressed well, ate at nice restaurants, bought expensive things, and even sent money to her mother, who was caring for her son in a city in the interior of the country.

Tina worked nights and had the days free. That was the kind of life Lilian wanted. If she could live as Tina did, she would use her time to finish her education.

"You can have everything I have," Tina assured her. "Let me explain."

And she did explain, in complete detail. The dark-skinned young woman with long hair and an enchanting smile worked in a nightclub. She stripped in front of the audience. Later, she encouraged the patrons to drink, and if she wanted to, she would go out with one of them for a reasonable sum of money.

At first Lilian wanted to have nothing to do with that life-style. Her dreams were a far cry from being a nightclub dancer. But as time passed and Lilian's financial situation worsened, Tina persisted. "Don't be stupid," she said. "It's the only way you can finish your education and fulfill your dream."

"I don't want that kind of life."

"But I'm not talking about life, girl. I'm talking about just for a while, so you can afford school."

In time, Lilian began to think she didn't have much to lose. She had been raped by her stepfather. Later, two boyfriends passed through her life who deceived her with false promises. And where had God been all that time? Why had He abandoned her? Why hadn't He taken care of her?

Tina's arrival at the club that night jerked Lilian out of her thoughts. "Finally, girl!" Tina said, almost shouting so she could be heard over the hellish noise. "I'll introduce you to Mauricio.

He's the owner of this club and a great guy. I've already told him about you, and he's willing to help you."

That was how everything began. After that night, Lilian's life turned completely around. She was pretty, with a captivating smile and big, black eyes full of mystery. At first she only danced on the stage and didn't go out with men or sell herself. However, she began to smoke and to drink, and after a time, she started to use drugs occasionally. But money was still scarce. More than once she thought that what she did at the club wasn't worth the little she earned.

"You don't have any money because you don't want it," Mauricio said one day. "If you're working here, you should do the whole thing. There are lots of guys willing to give you money."

Lilian didn't remember how it happened, but one day she woke up in a filthy motel room beside a man she had never seen before and whom she would never see again. That day she thought she had reached rock bottom. But five years passed quickly—years of loneliness, of despair, of anguish. At first the guilt was incessant. Her conscience condemned her all day long. She felt unclean. When she walked down the street, she felt as though everyone knew what she did for a living. And she never had enough money. At one point she had saved a bit, hoping to continue her studies in architecture. But then she was arrested and accused of murder. Two months later she was proven innocent and set free. However, the legal fees had consumed all the money she had saved.

The loss of her savings and of her dream of becoming an architect discouraged her completely. So, she threw herself headlong into a life of promiscuity. And perhaps she believed that she deserved the pain inflicted on her by her lifestyle; maybe it was a just punishment for her behavior. Year after year she sank lower, until there was nothing left of the girl with dreams, who had planned to live the low life only until she finished her education.

* * * * *

Early one Saturday morning, Lilian lay in a bed in a filthy motel room trying to sleep. Beside her lay a stranger who had paid her to spend the night with him. Lilian was crying silently. She was sadder and lonelier than ever. Her body was just an object that men bought.

Would anyone ever love her? Did she deserve to be loved? How had she reached this point? The questions depressed her, so she switched on the radio at the head of the bed, turning the volume down so as not to awaken the stranger.

Then an impressive sentence spoken by someone on the radio caught her attention. A preacher said, "You are the most important thing on earth to Jesus."

Lilian felt a shiver run through her body. She pressed her ear against the radio and continued listening.

> It doesn't matter where you are—whether in a hospital bed or traveling down a highway, in a prison cell or in a dirty motel room unable to sleep. I want you to know that Jesus loves you and died to save you. Please don't say that you aren't worth anything or that you don't deserve what He has done for you. Neither you nor I are worth anything. We didn't do anything to deserve Jesus' love. He just loves us.

The words seemed meant for her alone. She felt as though the preacher knew who she was and how she had been living. It was astonishing. She kept listening.

What do you need to do to make Jesus' love real in your life? "If we confess our sins, He is faithful and just to forgive us our sins and to cleanse us from all unrighteousness" [1 John 1:9].

In order to confess, we must recognize that we have sinned. We must also accept the fact that we can't fix the situation on our own. What good can medicine do people who don't admit that they are sick and won't take the medicine? Christ's love is the remedy for everything bad, but sinners must recognize their condition and confess their sins.

> To whom should they confess? David wrote,
> I acknowledged my sin to You,
> And my iniquity I have not hidden.
> I said, "I will confess my transgressions to the LORD,"
> And You forgave the iniquity of my sin [Psalm 32:5].

The voice continued.

We don't need to confess our sins to another human being. God is the only One who can forgive us. He is the only One we should turn to. "If anyone sins, we have an Advocate with the Father, Jesus Christ the righteous" [1 John 2:1]. Why look only to Jesus? "Nor is there salvation in any other, for there is no other name under heaven given among men by which we must be saved" [Acts 4:12].

Lilian felt more astonished by the minute. She had always thought that the saints could mediate for her, but she learned that the Bible says "there is one God and one Mediator between God and men, the Man Christ Jesus" (1 Timothy 2:5).

Jesus is the only Mediator between God and human beings. That's because only Jesus can fully understand human beings. Only He went through the valley of pain and suffering. "We do not have a High Priest who cannot sympathize with our weaknesses, but was in all points tempted as we are, yet without sin," Paul said, speaking of Jesus. "Let us therefore come boldly to the throne of grace, that we may obtain mercy and find grace to help in time of need" (Hebrews 4:15, 16).

The thought that Jesus, the Son of God, could understand her amazed Lilian. But that is what the voice on the radio was saying.

The preacher continued.

That terribly dark afternoon on Calvary, the Lord Jesus was not dying because He had sinned. He had lived a holy life in spite of having been tempted. That afternoon Jesus gave His life for you and for me. It was you and I who deserved to die. You and I are the ones who followed our own ways.

But He was wounded for our transgressions,
He was bruised for our iniquities;
The chastisement for our peace was upon Him,
And by His stripes we are healed. [Isaiah 53:5].

Come with me to Calvary. Close your eyes and imagine that scene of pain and death. Watch the Lord Jesus hanging from the wretched cross. Watch Him bleed. See the thorns that wound His forehead. Listen to the scoffing of His killers.

Did Jesus deserve to die there like a criminal? No. But He loves you. That's why He was willing to die. You may have lived the worst of lives. You may have sunken into the darkest depths of sin. You may have destroyed everything good that you once had and feel like trash right now. Listen to me closely: in spite of all that, you are still the most precious thing Jesus has. Otherwise, He would never have died on the cross for you.

The radio preacher concluded with this appeal:

How could you possibly think He doesn't understand you? How could you think He doesn't know how you feel? He loves you and right now is standing with His arms open, waiting for you to give yourself to Him.

Lilian thought she was going crazy. It couldn't be true. How could that man on the radio know exactly how she was feeling? She cried. She cried a lot. She cried as though her tears could wash her inner world clean.

When the speaker finished his appeal, an announcer came on and said, "Pastor Bullón, who has just presented this message, will be preaching today at eleven A.M. in the stadium in this city."

The news filled Lilian with joy. She decided she would go to the stadium to see the man who had spoken on the radio and hear more about the love of Jesus.

When the stranger beside her got up, he asked, "Where do you want me to drop you off?"

"I want to go to the stadium," Lilian replied.

When she got out of the car at the stadium, she noticed that many people were hurrying into it. She joined the crowd. She'd been there once before—for a concert by a famous musical group. Lilian liked music. That Saturday morning she was captivated by the hymns being sung by a huge choir.

Lilian noticed that the people congregated in the stadium that morning differed from those she knew. There was a special brilliance in their eyes. They sang happily. And when they looked at her, their faces spoke of peace.

* * * * *

At eleven o'clock sharp, I stood up behind the pulpit with my Bible open. I never start preaching without reading a Bible text. The Bible clearly states,

> By the word of the LORD the heavens were made,
> And all the host of them by the breath of His
>   mouth. . . .
> For He spoke, and it was done;
> He commanded, and it stood fast (Psalm 33:6, 9).

And when Jesus was on this earth, the power of His word enabled the paralyzed to walk, opened blind eyes, and even resurrected dead people. There is power in God's Word. It can create, and it can restore. I've learned this over my lifetime.

That morning the Word of God worked a miracle in Lilian. The subject of the love of God captivated her heart, which had almost been destroyed by the bad decisions she had made. The scripture reading that day was

> He who covers his sins will not prosper,
> But whoever confesses and forsakes them will have
>   mercy (Proverbs 28:13).

Everyone wants to be forgiven, and many people confess their sins. However, few wish to forsake them. Yet to receive salvation we must both confess our sins and repent of them. Many people confuse repentance with regret, which is merely fear of suffering the consequences of sin. To repent is to feel pain for having hurt God's heart and to want your life to be changed.

When Jesus walked among men, He said, " 'I did not come to call the righteous, but sinners, to repentance' " (Matthew 9:13). His appeal to repentance is an appeal to sinners. It comes to those who are tired of struggling for a better life. Those who don't have peace in their hearts. Those who feel useless. It is an appeal to those who feel defeated and rejected by society. Lilian felt like that.

Lilian wondered what she must do in order to repent. The answer came from the Bible. It says that the goodness of God leads us to repentance. (See Romans 2:4.) It is God's love that moves us to repent. You can't manufacture repentance yourself. Your heart won't naturally give birth to it—it is born of divine love. You only have to accept the fact that when God asks you to abandon sin and come to Him, it is because He wants His promises to become a reality in your life. "The Lord is not slack concerning His promise, as some count slackness, but is long-suffering toward us, not willing that any should perish but that all should come to repentance" (2 Peter 3:9).

As Lilian sat in that stadium, she cried in repentance. Her pain didn't come from what she had suffered. She cried because of the choices she had made. But her heart was also lacerated by the question "Why am I only now hearing about the love of God?"

My voice brought her back to the present: "Today is the day of good news; today is the day of salvation."

This was it. Today she had the opportunity to begin a new life.

"Come to Jesus now," I continued. "Come just as you are, without promises. Bring Jesus the broken pieces of your life so He can rebuild it. Bring Him your empty heart so He can give meaning to your existence. Bring Him the stained pages of your life, and receive from His hand clean pages on which to write a new story."

Lilian struggled. She didn't want to make a hasty decision, to be carried away only by the emotion of the moment. She saw dozens of people going toward the platform. Finally, she could no longer resist the voice of the Holy Spirit, and she gave herself to Jesus.

The last verse read in that service was "Repent therefore and be converted, that your sins may be blotted out, so that times of refreshing may come from the presence of the Lord" (Acts 3:19).

Refreshing. That is what Lilian felt as she left the stadium that afternoon. In spite of the implacable heat of that December day south of the equator, she felt a soft breeze caressing her face like the sweet kiss of Jesus' forgiveness.

*   *   *   *   *

Many years later I was holding evangelistic meetings in that same city. I had preached the evening's sermon one rainy night and was waiting in the lobby of the hall for the person who was to drive me back to my hotel. While I was sitting there, one of my colleagues came in and said, "There's a woman here who would like to greet you."

"All right," I replied.

An elegant woman appeared before the words were out of my mouth. I didn't know who she was; I had never seen her before. But it was apparent that her emotions had been stirred.

This woman asked anxiously, "Could I talk to you for a bit tomorrow? I have a very interesting story, and you have a lot to do with it, but I see that you are ready to leave right now."

The next day we had a conversation. She was a very well-known and respected architect, and a happily married woman with two children. She was the fruit of the love of God. In a word, she was Lilian.

CHAPTER THREE

A Cold Night in August

It was a typical August night in São Paulo—rainy, cold, and foggy. But Juliano's sadness had nothing to do with the weather. His pain was born from his life, if one could say he had a life.

Juliano had just beaten up his wife—again. Lately, it was happening more frequently and that depressed him. Juliano loved his wife, even though she no longer believed it. He had always loved her, ever since the day he saw her for the first time at a volleyball tournament. Then, Juliano had been a young engineer, just twenty-five years old, full of ambitious dreams and plans. And Laura was a beautiful volleyball player in the junior division of a famous Brazilian team. Within a year they were married.

For the first ten years of their marriage, life seemed to smile on them. Juliano received the offer of an excellent job in Europe, which he accepted. Without a second thought, Laura abandoned her career in sports to accompany him. Two years later a son was born to them. And then the arrival of a beautiful baby girl with golden curls completed their joy.

Eventually, they returned to their home country. There, Juliano continued working for the company that had employed him in Europe, and Laura threw herself into being a full-time homemaker. They had plenty of money and lived in a pretty mansion in one of the more sophisticated parts of the city. They frequented the circles of high society, enrolled their children in the best schools, and watched them grow. But anyone who saw Juliano that August night—walking with his head down and with his hands shoved deep into the pockets of his leather overcoat—would have never imagined that he was someone who apparently had every reason to be happy.

As Juliano walked slowly along, scenes of violence in which he was the perpetrator paraded through his mind. He thought himself the worst specimen of the human race. He cried silently so the people walking wouldn't notice. He cried because of the pain of just living, because of the absurdity of his beating the woman he loved, because of the tragedy of seeing his children destroyed. He wept because of his weakness, because of his humiliating subservience to alcohol—though he refused to admit his addiction.

Juliano considered himself just a social drinker. The truth was that he drank every day. He had to. Without alcohol, he felt insecure, fragile, indecisive. When he drank, everything changed. He felt like the king of the world, and he became aggressive.

He had promised Laura that he would take her to dinner at a fancy restaurant that night. When she came down from her room looking beautiful in a fetching black dress, she found him drinking. Guessing that the promise of dinner had evaporated, she sighed deeply, settled onto a sofa, and said, "This again? Do you suppose it will ever end? Couldn't you have at least told me you didn't want to go out? Why did you make me get all dressed up for nothing?"

That did it. Juliano had pushed the bottle of whiskey aside and let his anger overcome him. Later, when Laura had shut herself in her room, crying, he had gone out to wander in the night.

While Juliano walked, he thought of the daughter he hadn't seen in months. He had kicked her out of the house when she became pregnant at seventeen. Now, although he would never have admitted it, he felt guilty. What kind of a father was he, anyway? His heart urged him to find his daughter and bring her home, but his pride was bigger, moralistic, rigid.

Juliano's son was completely immersed in drugs. Juliano had tried everything he could think of to save him from the grip of the terrible vice. He had talked firmly though lovingly. He had punished him. He had paid for the best specialists and the best rehabilitation clinics. Nothing had helped. That made him frustrated, and he found solace only in alcohol. He blamed his children for his own failures and defeats—until he remembered that he had started drinking when they were still small. What had happened to him wasn't their fault.

What can people do in circumstances like these? Where can they go? Juliano felt like he was in a dead-end tunnel. Or, he thought, maybe it was more like falling into an abyss from which he couldn't escape.

To make things worse, Juliano was a rationalist. He didn't consider himself an atheist; he believed in God. But he thought God was some kind of motivating force and nothing more. He couldn't fathom the idea of a personal God who was interested in people and who was capable of intervening in their lives. The cultures of the university and of Europe had completely destroyed his ability to believe in spiritual things. He believed in things he could see and touch. He was a pragmatist. That pragmatism had helped him professionally. But it left no place in his life for God. Anyway, hadn't he obtained success, wealth, and social status without any help from God?

Sometimes when Juliano was all alone, he admitted to himself that he was an empty man, and he asked himself what good it had done him to have accomplished so much in life when he wasn't happy. What was happiness, anyway? He didn't know how to define it, although he was sure it wasn't what he had been living for the past few years. He felt like a failure as a husband and father. If he couldn't make the people he loved happy, what was the point of living?

These thoughts had surfaced in his mind often. Every time they came, he shook his head and pretended everything was OK.

* * * * *

The sight of crowds of people crossing the street and entering the city coliseum shook Juliano out of his internal whirlwind. He asked one of the passersby what was happening.

"It's an evangelistic meeting. A preacher is giving inspiring messages," the man said while hurrying on toward the coliseum.

A preacher? Juliano had heard about evangelists before, but he had never had contact with any. He thought preachers were deceitful—that they took advantage of people who were emotionally vulnerable. However, that night Juliano had nothing to do other than to wander around while he tried to forget that he had beaten his wife. He felt curious. What did preachers say? There must be some reason why thousands of people were entering the coliseum. He decided to find out.

Juliano found a place on the upper level directly across from the stage. There were huge speakers and a lighting system that rivaled those of the best of shows. Soft instrumental music mingled with the noise made by the crowds of people who were looking for seats.

In a few minutes the coliseum was full, and a musical group came onto the stage. Juliano tried to ignore them. He wanted to avoid being influenced by any of the preliminaries. He was there only as a critical observer, intending to discover how preachers manipulate the minds of their audiences.

However, when the group began to sing, the words of their song captured his attention. They spoke of forgiveness, of love, of a new opportunity in life. The words and music touched Juliano's heart. But he was a rationalist. He couldn't permit himself the luxury of listening to his heart.

Half an hour later the preacher stepped forward and read from the Bible—from chapter 3 of the Gospel of John. The passage told about a man named Nicodemus who sought the Lord Jesus one night. The story caught Juliano's interest.

Nicodemus was a rich man in an enviable social position. He had been successful in his professional career and was widely admired. But when night came, he couldn't sleep. He tossed from side to side on his bed. Insomnia threw permanent shadows on his life. He felt empty and didn't understand why. He wasn't doing anything bad to anyone—he wasn't stealing or murdering or committing adultery—yet he wasn't happy. What was missing? Why did he have this feeling that he was smothering this deep fear that never left him in peace?

On one of those sleepless nights, Nicodemus got up and went looking for Jesus. When he left his house that night, he planned to fall at Jesus' feet and say, "Oh Lord, please help me. I'm lost." But how could he do that? He was one of the religious leaders of the Jewish nation. Religious leaders tend to think they're in this world to help, not to ask for help. So,

Nicodemus's pride spoke before his heart, and he said to Jesus, " 'Rabbi, we know that You are a teacher come from God; for no one can do these signs that You do unless God is with him' " (John 3:2).

Jesus knew that Nicodemus could pretend that everything was just fine. He knew that he could tell himself a thousand times that he needed nothing. But Jesus also knew that behind that facade of a winner, there was a poor, unhappy, failed man who was struggling with life. So, Jesus went right to the point. He said, " 'Most assuredly, I say to you, unless one is born again, he cannot see the kingdom of God' " (John 3:3).

The Lord Jesus was talking about a new birth. A new beginning. A blank page upon which to write a new story. That is what Juliano needed. If he could erase the story that he had written up to that point, he would do a lot of things differently.

In spite of the size of the crowd in the huge auditorium, you could have heard a pin drop. Thousands of people were seeking answers to their spiritual uncertainties. The message awakened an interest in Juliano too. He concentrated on every word the preacher said.

*   *   *   *   *

Why is a new birth necessary? What kind of birth is it? The preacher read from the prophet Isaiah:

> The whole head is sick,
> And the whole heart faints.
> From the sole of the foot even to the head,
> There is no soundness in it,
> But wounds and bruises and putrefying sores (Isaiah
>   1:5, 6).

When gangrene starts devouring an arm or a leg, that limb must be amputated before the terrible disease destroys the whole body. Isaiah wrote of a whole body overcome by gangrene. There is nothing to amputate—the whole thing is rotten. There is no remedy for this kind of body. It is condemned to death. The apostle Paul wrote, "All have sinned and fall short of the glory of God" (Romans 3:23). He was saying that human beings come into this world with a bent toward sin. Similarly, David declared,

> Behold, I was brought forth in iniquity,
> And in sin my mother conceived me (Psalm 51:5).

Then Paul stated the outcome of the human situation. He wrote, "The wages of sin is death" (Romans 6:23).

What Juliano was hearing knocked down the philosophy on which he had built his life. He had always considered himself a good man with commendable morals, such as honesty, punctuality, and trustworthiness. The preacher was challenging his view of himself. He was saying that people are evil by nature. They may acquire some moral values through education and cultural formation, but human nature is flawed and bent toward wrong. That also means they can't, on their own, understand spiritual truths. That is why Paul stated that people naturally "walk, in the futility of their mind, having their understanding darkened, being alienated from the life of God, because of the ignorance that is in them, because of the blindness of their heart" (Ephesians 4:17, 18).

"Alienated from the life of God." What a startling phrase! Does that mean another type of life exists that the natural human being is ignorant of? Exactly. Jesus Himself said, " 'I have come that they might have life, and that they may have it more abundantly' " (John 10:10).

43

Where is this abundant life that Jesus talked about? Juliano was an unhappy, empty, hopeless man. He loved his family, and yet he was destroying them. What kind of life made him go whole nights without sleeping? Lately, he felt like a walking corpse—dead, yet still alive. Now the preacher stated emphatically, "Even when we were dead in trespasses [sins]," God "made us alive together with Christ" (Ephesians 2:5).

Juliano felt his critical attitude changing into one of interest. Then he heard the preacher say, "I want you to remember what I am going to tell you. Your life is destroyed even if you won't admit it. Where are the dreams you had? What did you do with the wonderful family God gave you? You have destroyed it all. You are an empty, hopeless man. You are a prisoner in the grip of alcoholism, and you don't have the strength to overcome it."

Juliano trembled. The preacher was undressing him in public! His spirit rebelled. "I won't listen to this!" he said and started out of the auditorium.

However, as he left, he could still hear the preacher's voice: ". . . but God loves you. You are the most precious thing He has in this life. Oh, how He loves you! You didn't do anything to deserve it, but He loves you anyway. You can close your ears and run, but you will never manage to make God stop loving you."

Juliano tried desperately to escape. He ran like a madman. But the last words he heard continued to ring in his ears:

Can the Ethiopian change his skin or the leopard its spots?
Then may you also do good who are accustomed to do evil
(Jeremiah 13:23).

It was the truth even if he hated to admit it. He knew he was proud—arrogant. He had tried to change himself many times, but all his efforts had been useless. There was nothing he could do to change the situation.

The Bible is right. We must be born again. Jesus said as much to Nicodemus: " 'That which is born of the flesh is flesh, and that which is born of the Spirit is spirit' " (John 3:6). Jesus was talking about *spiritual* birth. A new mind and a new heart. New motivations. A new direction in life. This new birth is called conversion. It is more than merely a change in the way one thinks; it's a life change. It isn't just a matter of improving the old way of life. It is finding a completely new way to live—a turnabout, a 180-degree switch.

How does this new birth happen? If a physical birth is a miracle, a spiritual birth is an even greater miracle. Even though it is miraculous, however, it is a real experience. It happens at the moment when a created being, tired of struggling, recognizes that he is helpless and calls on God with all the strength of his heart.

God needs only a second to implant a new nature in the human heart. People's resistance to accepting Him may mean that working out the new birth in their life will take some time. It also takes time to get used to the new nature. Theologically, this is called sanctification. But the new birth takes place instantaneously. For some, it may be a dramatic event. For others, it may be almost imperceptible. But the results are visible. They are born of a heart filled with the peace of divine forgiveness.

* * * * *

After Juliano left the coliseum that cold Saturday night, he began to run. Anyone who saw him might have thought he was running from the police. But he was running away—or at least trying to run away—from the Holy Spirit. He was struggling to forget what he had heard, but the words pursued him. They seemed to explode inside his mind. The words that made the deepest impact were the preacher's assurances that "God loves you. You are the most precious thing He has in this life. . . . You didn't do anything to deserve it, but He loves you anyway. You can close your ears and run, but you will never manage to make God stop loving you."

When a red traffic light made Juliano stop running, he looked up at the sky. There was no moon nor stars, only dense fog and a fine drizzle. *God,* he cried out silently, *that man says You love me. How can You love me? Look at my life. I'm worthless. I'm just a complete failure as a human being—as a husband and father. How can You love me?*

Juliano heard within his heart what seemed like a Voice that said, *"Son, don't ask how I can love you. Just accept that I do."*

On that street corner, Juliano cried in silence. He told God the story of his life, and he opened his heart and begged for help. And God worked the miracle. Juliano was born again.

After that miraculous rebirth, he walked through the city for a long time, talking with God. It was early morning when he got home and went into his bedroom. Laura was still awake, but she pretended to be sleeping.

Juliano lay down in the bed. But before he went to sleep, he did something that he hadn't done for many years: he placed a sweet kiss on Laura's forehead. She cried while he slept.

The next morning, Laura found Juliano dumping all the alcoholic beverages in the house into the toilet. "Are you crazy?" she asked.

Juliano stopped for a moment and looked at her, and Laura saw an expression on his face just like the one she had seen years before, when he brought a rose to her after that volleyball game.

"Forgive me," he said in a voice charged with love and sincerity. "Forgive me for what I have done to you, for the pain I have caused you, for my indifference and brutality."

Laura had never before seen her husband so moved. Many thoughts ran through her mind. *What is happening to him? Why this sudden change? What is he up to?*

Juliano's voice brought her thoughts back to the moment. "Will you give me another chance to make you happy?" he said.

"What is wrong with you?" she asked anxiously.

"Everything, but nothing. I've been born again. I'm a new man."

"What do you mean, 'a new man'? Explain that. Something strange has happened to you, and I want to know what it is." She was intrigued. Something mysterious *had* happened—or else Juliano was donning a mask of goodness to hide something.

"Do you believe that God loves me?"

Juliano's question surprised her. "Of course! I mean, I think so," she replied.

"Don't think so. Be sure of it. God loves me!"

"But . . . what does that have to do with your strange behavior?"

"Don't you understand? I've been born again. The man who hurt you is dead. I'm a new person!"

Laura was confused. She didn't understand. But whatever had happened to her husband was good. This definitely wasn't the same Juliano who had beaten her in a drunken fury the night before.

Juliano walked over and sat on the edge of the bed. Then he told Laura what had happened to him. Together, they surveyed their lives. They talked about their children. And then they embraced tenderly, and she promised to go with him to the coliseum that night.

*   *   *   *   *

More than two decades after that cold August night I was eating lunch with a group of friends when a beautiful, smiling woman and a handsome man dressed in a dark-blue suit walked toward me. Their faces were shining with happiness.

The man hugged me and whispered in my ear. "Thank you for your message that night," he said. "Thank you for introducing me to Jesus." He was a happy man. His son had accepted Jesus Christ and was freed from the grip of drugs. And he had searched tirelessly for his daughter until he found her and brought her back into the family. That's how it is with Jesus. That's why the Bible says, "If anyone is in Christ, he is a new creation; old things have passed away; behold, all things have become new" (2 Corinthians 5:17).

This man had been transformed by the wonderful grace of Christ. He was Juliano.

CHAPTER FOUR

A Conflicted Priest

The sun was dying majestically in the countryside of southern Chile. A nine-year-old boy sat absorbed in contemplation of the impressive scene. The sunset was like a work of art, a beautiful picture painted by some famous artist—only the picture was real, the colors were alive. The beauty of the evening was supernatural, an invitation to reflection and worship.

Unconsciously, the boy knelt, and his thoughts, till then focused on the fiery orange horizon, became lost in infinity. He flew on the wings of his imagination to an imposing cathedral overflowing with multitudes of people. The boy imagined himself as an adult dressed in priestly robes and officiating at the Mass.

Sixto didn't know when he first felt the calling to become a priest. But that evening as he knelt on the hillside, the conviction that he had been born to be a servant of God pressed deep into his heart.

At suppertime, as Sixto sat at the table and the warmth from the stove softened the cold winter air, he spoke to the two women who sat there with him. "I want to be a priest, and I hope you will help me enroll in the seminary," he told them.

"Praised be the virgin," his grandmother exclaimed and crossed herself twice.

Sixto had a wonderful Christian family comprised of himself, his mother, and his grandmother. The two women were fervent Catholics; they never missed Mass for any reason. They arranged for Sixto to work as an assistant to the parish priest, helping with the duties of the Sunday services.

The lad was fascinated by the mysteries of religion. He was calm and obedient, and a sort of mysticism adorned his actions. Everyone who knew him liked him and believed that God intended him for something religious. With the help of the parish priest, Sixto enrolled in a Jesuit seminary. By the time he was twenty-two years old, he was an ordained priest with a parish of his own to tend.

In Sixto's studies at the seminary, he had learned to think analytically. And he had grown to love theology. It provided him with the arguments he used to defend Catholic dogmas with firmness and conviction. But while he was studying theology, he began to be troubled by doubt. He loved the virgin Mary and considered her not only a saint but also humanity's intercessor before God. Not only his reasoning but also his emotions were bound up in this dogma. So a statement that he found in the Bible shocked him: "There is one God, and one Mediator between God and men, the Man Christ Jesus" (1 Timothy 2:5). Something was wrong either with the Bible or with the dogma.

Sixto chose not to think about it. He feared that doubt would diminish his love for God. So, despite his analytical orientation, he decided to submit himself to the doctrine and to ignore his concerns about the conflict. He accepted the tradition affirmed by the church, even though this attitude didn't fit his personality. In doing so, he felt like he was breaking something inside of him.

Years later, doubts began to surface again. He'd become aware of so many contradictions between the Bible and church traditions that he felt he couldn't be sincere and still ignore them. The question was, Which was right, the Bible or the church? Or did the Bible authorize the church to change the Bible's teachings? These questions led Sixto to study the Bible more deeply.

As he began to study, he searched first of all to find out why he should believe that the Bible is the Word of God. He discovered that the apostle Paul had declared categorically, "All Scripture is given by inspiration of God, and is profitable for doctrine, for reproof, for correction, for instruction in righteousness" (2 Timothy 3:16). In saying that "all Scripture is given by inspiration of God," the apostle was declaring that even though the writers of the Bible were human beings, the message they recorded came from God. The apostle Peter wrote, "Prophecy never came by the will of man, but holy men of God spoke as they were moved by the Holy Spirit" (2 Peter 1:21).

Sixto felt like a sinner for even having questions about his religion. He spent entire nights in meditation and prayer, asking the virgin for forgiveness for doubting her. He fasted frequently and regularly performed acts of penitence, reasoning that his doubts were no more than passing temptations that would disappear in time. But his mind was like a seething volcano that was ready to explode.

* * * * *

Five years into Sixto's ministry, two things happened that unsettled his life. First, he met Ana, a faithful, young Catholic woman. Their conversations centered on religious and devotional themes. Eventually, the young priest began sharing his theological doubts with her. His heart told him he could trust her.

"Do you think the Bible is the Word of God?" he asked her one day, his voice charged with emotion.

"Of course," she responded. "How could I possibly doubt it?"

"Do you think the Bible's authority is superior to any human teaching?"

"Absolutely!"

"Is it possible that over time some parts of the Bible could become obsolete, making it necessary for the church to bring it up-to-date?"

Ana shrugged her shoulders. She didn't know the answer, but the question made her begin to worry about Father Sixto and the uncertainty he apparently felt about fundamental points of the Catholic faith. However, she agreed to study the Bible with him.

As they studied, they found verses that, rather than clearing up Father Sixto's doubts, confused him even more.

> "The grass withers, the flower fades,
> But the word of our God stands forever" (Isaiah 40:8).

The prophet Isaiah said. So, the eternity of God's Word was unquestionable. And Paul declared that Jesus Christ, God in human flesh, "is the same yesterday, today, and forever" (Hebrews 13:8). So if God is eternal and His Word is unchanging, what about Paul's statement that Jesus is the only Mediator between God and human beings? At what point did this stop being true? When did the virgin Mary begin to intercede for them as well?

What troubled Sixto most was not the question of whether or not to accept the virgin Mary as a mediator. Rather, it was the matter of the authority of the Bible as the Word of God. The question about the virgin's mediation was just a corollary to something much more serious. If people could modify God's Word, then what was to prevent human errors from creeping in?

One Sunday, Sixto shared some of his doubts with his congregation during Mass. That occasioned a call from the bishop. "You can't be confusing the church like that," he warned Sixto. "People come to Mass to be nourished, not to be confused by your personal doubts."

"But my doubts aren't personal," Sixto protested. "What we teach contradicts what the Bible says. All Christians should wonder about these things."

A sepulchral silence followed as the bishop stared at Sixto wide-eyed, unblinking, unable to believe what he was hearing.

"I can't be sincere while stifling my convictions," Sixto said, breaking the silence. He felt like a child who had been caught doing something naughty.

"You don't have convictions, Father. What you have are doubts, temptations, a lack of confidence in the dogmas of the church. We'll give you six months to think about it. You must spend the time in fasting, penances, and prayers. And you must remain in seclusion; your functions as a priest will be suspended."

Sixto went into seclusion and spent six long months in prayer and Bible study. It was during this time that the second event that changed his life took place. Sixto took into seclusion with him a book by Martin Luther on the subject of faith. A Lutheran pastor had given him the book while they were both serving as chaplains in the Chilean army. Sixto's reading of the book and his biblical research convinced him that the sacrament of penance had no place in Christian experience. Salvation is not by works. It can be obtained only by grace. As the apostle Paul declared, "By grace you have been saved through faith, and that not of yourselves; it is the gift of God, not of works, lest anyone should boast" (Ephesians 2:8, 9).

What purpose, then, did penance serve? And why did the church teach something that wasn't biblical? These questions brought him back to the problem of biblical authority.

Sixto sought to discover evidence for the inspiration of the Bible outside of the statements of the biblical authors themselves. The Holy Spirit guided him to three conclusions. First, the Bible was written during a span of some fifteen hundred years. Moses, the author of the first book, never met John, the author of the last book. Hosea didn't know Ezra, nor did Matthew know Isaiah, nor Luke know Jeremiah. Yet all these men wrote essentially the same message. It was almost as if one day the forty Bible writers had sat down and decided what each one would write so they could turn out a book with unbroken unity of theme and message. This unity in itself proves that the Divine Mind was at work behind each of the Bible writers, inspiring them to record God's message to human beings.

Second, the exactness with which biblical prophecies have been fulfilled witnesses to the inspiration of the Bible. The Bible contains many prophecies Sixto didn't understand—such as those in Daniel and Revelation. But the fulfillment of other prophecies in Scripture confirmed his faith in its divine inspiration. And not only have its prophecies been fulfilled, but it is supernaturally accurate scientifically as well. For instance, Isaiah wrote that God "sits above the *circle* of the earth" (Isaiah 40:22; emphasis added). The scientists of Isaiah's day believed that the earth was flat and square, yet the Bible said it is round. On October 12, 1492, Christopher Columbus proved that the Bible is right.

Third, the many stories Sixto had heard about the transforming power of the Bible did more than move his heart. To his mind, they constituted evidence of the Bible's divine nature. In fact, he himself had begun to feel at peace only when he was reading Scripture. It was as if God Himself were speaking in each word, saying, "Son, let Me guide you through the paths of life. Let Me lead your feet in the ways of righteousness."

Those six months of suspension seemed like an eternity to Sixto. They were filled with days and nights of intense mental and spiritual anguish. He had always trusted the teachings of the Fathers. Now, though he was a priest, the more he studied the Bible, the less he trusted the church and its teachings. He couldn't deny the Bible's authority nor the importance of Bible study.

One day, as he was reading a story in the book of Acts, he found a verse that compared the people who lived in Berea with those who lived in Thessalonica. It says that the Bereans "were more fair-minded than those in Thessalonica, in that they received the word with all readiness, and searched the Scriptures daily to find out whether these things were so" (Acts 17:11).

Luke stated that the Bereans were more "fair-minded." Luke wrote his Gospel in Greek, and the Greek word translated here as "fair-minded" is *eugenesteros*. It means having a sharper, more intelligent mind; a mind that doesn't allow one to be deceived. The Bereans were more fair-minded in two ways. They *received* the Word, and then they *searched* it—they analyzed it with a single purpose: to find out whether the things Paul was preaching to them were so.

The Christians at Berea wanted to understand God's will. They didn't simply accept what other people—even trusted religious leaders such as Paul—told them. They wanted to find out for themselves whether what they were being taught was really found in the sacred Scriptures. That's why they went down in history as being "more fair-minded."

This passage brought comfort to Sixto's heart because, contrary to the bishop's accusation, he wasn't "unsure," "full of doubt," or "lacking in faith." Rather, the Bible called him more fair-minded precisely because he wanted to know "whether these things were so."

*   *   *   *   *

When the months of spiritual seclusion ended, Sixto's heart no longer doubted. He knew what he was going to do. He presented himself before the bishop again.

"I hope you have reflected sufficiently and that your doubts have disappeared," the bishop said severely.

Sixto didn't want to be discourteous. Despite his discoveries during the months of seclusion, he still respected the church and its authorities. For that reason, though, he spoke firmly, his voice was gentle. He said, "I've reached a conclusion: If I want to be honest with God, with the church, and with myself, I cannot continue being a Catholic priest. I'm willing to renounce my priestly duties and accept all the consequences that my decision implies."

The bishop's eyes looked like balls of fire. "Is that your final word?" he asked.

"Yes, sir. I don't need any more time to think. I've made my decision."

It seemed that short conversation crushed all of Sixto's fondest dreams. The young priest knew what awaited him. His life wouldn't be easy after this. How would he break the news to his mother and grandmother? And how would he survive the future when his entire life he had imagined being a priest? The priest-hood was his vocation, his soul, his only objective in life.

It wasn't the material difficulties that Sixto would now face that bothered him—the question of what occupation he would take up, of how he would support himself. His worries had more to do with heart matters. Even though his mind told him he had made the right choice, his heart refused to accept it. However, he took three things with him when he left the monastery: his Bible, the book by Martin Luther, and the deep conviction that, even if at the moment he was suffering deeply, he must continue discovering the wonders of God's Word.

He would keep studying. He was sure God's Spirit would guide him to the truth, and the truth would finally set him free.

* * * *

Ana had never stopped thinking about Father Sixto's anxiet-ies and doubts. When he suddenly disappeared from the parish, she asked about him and found that he had been deprived of his priestly functions and gone into seclusion in a Franciscan mon-astery to meditate and reflect.

During the months that followed, she heard nothing more about him. But she didn't forget him. Every day, at the hour of the evening Mass, she mentioned the young priest in her prayers. She was aware of the spiritual struggle he was facing. She knew he was a sincere man and that the doubts that tormented him were the result of his sincerity and honesty.

In time, Ana began thinking she would never see Sixto again. Then one cool morning in July, as she was returning from the bakery with a bag of pastries, she saw him. She could hardly believe her eyes. He wasn't wearing his robe. Instead, he was dressed in blue jeans and a checkered flannel shirt.

They hugged briefly and then she asked, "What has become of you, Father?"

"Well, here I am, back again."

"You're different. What happened to you?"

It was true. He was different. Burdened by a thousand concerns, he was no longer the confident young man, sure of himself and full of hopes for the future. But he still valued the Bible. So, after exchanging news, they agreed on a time to meet to study the Bible together. They would begin that afternoon in Ana's house.

Ana didn't tire of asking questions. To answer them, Sixto would open his Bible and read one verse after another. "Look what David says," he observed.

> Your word is a lamp to my feet
> And a light to my path (Psalm 119:105).

"God's Word is a light. Where there is light, there cannot be doubts. Things should be clear. That clarity can be found only in the Bible."

"Well, I've always read the Bible, but I don't understand it," Ana protested.

"That is because you read it by yourself. Many times people need help understanding it. Take the Ethiopian, for example. Luke wrote that one day this man was traveling from Jerusalem to Gaza and reading the Bible as he rode along in his chariot. 'So Philip ran to him, and heard him reading the prophet Isaiah, and said, "Do you understand what you are reading?" And he said, "How can I, unless someone guides me?" ' " (Acts 8:30, 31).

"Does that mean we should study the Bible together? Will you help me?"

"Of course!" Sixto responded. "If we're sincere, God will help us to find the truth. Look at what the apostle Paul says: 'These things we also speak, not in words which man's wisdom teaches but which the Holy Spirit teaches, comparing spiritual things with spiritual. But the natural man does not receive the things of the Spirit of God, for they are foolishness to him; nor can he know them, because they are spiritually discerned' " (1 Corinthians 2:13, 14).

From that day on, Ana and Sixto met twice a week to study the Bible. Time passed, and without realizing it, the two young people began to fall in love. One day Sixto looked deep into Ana's eyes and touched her hand with his own trembling hand. Then he said, "Anita, I'm in love with you. I think I always have been, even when I was a priest. Then, it was a forbidden feeling. Now, I can tell you: I love you!"

Ana's eyes filled with tears. Her heart too had suggested that feeling, but she had quickly quelled it. She thought she was just dreaming, that it was all a figment of her imagination.

Sixto waited for her to say something. But there are times when no words need to be spoken. Ana said it all with her eyes. Two years later they were married.

*   *   *   *   *

Eighteen years passed—years during which God guided Sixto and Ana into discovering many Bible truths. He also blessed them with two handsome sons and all the material goods they needed for life. They could have felt completely happy—except for one small problem. Sixto became spiritually unsettled once again. Many of his nights were sleepless, he was often grumpy, and he argued frequently with his wife and sons. And no one, not even Sixto himself, could understand exactly what was happening.

Sixto knew that God has a remnant of believers somewhere on this earth. While studying the book of Revelation, he had found the verse that says, "The dragon was roth with the woman, and went to make war with the remnant of her seed, which keep the commandments of God, and have the testimony of Jesus Christ" (Revelation 12:17, KJV).

This verse particularly perturbed Sixto. He knew that the woman it mentions represents God's church. So he concluded that some "seed" of that church must exist in the present time. There must be a remnant of believers. God's true church couldn't have disappeared completely.

Once Sixto concluded that God's true church must exist somewhere, he knew that he had to find it. But how would he know when he had found it?

According to Revelation 14:12, the remnant church would have two characteristics: its members would believe in Jesus Christ, and they would keep God's commandments.

Studying further, Sixto discovered the commandments of God in Exodus 20. But then he asked himself, *Isn't that all history? Didn't Jesus end all our concerns with those commandments when He died on Calvary?*

Sixto's internal struggle left him completely disconcerted. It wasn't only a mental conflict but one that also affected his emotions and, consequently, his relationships with other people— particularly his family and friends. It also affected him professionally, and as a result, Sixto and Ana started having financial problems.

One night Ana confronted Sixto. "We have to find some direction for our lives," she said. "We just cannot keep on the way we're going."

"You're not satisfied?" Sixto asked sarcastically.

"You know what I'm talking about. We've been happy for

eighteen years. The whole time I have stood beside you in the good and the bad. But lately you've become awfully hard to live with. You're nervous and grouchy, and worst of all, you're becoming careless in your duties as the head of our family."

Sixto knew his wife was right. He didn't have the strength to deal with the conflict he was feeling; it was practically paralyzing him. However, it was in those desperate circumstances that he finally found what he was searching for.

One night in September he was sitting on the couch searching through the various channels on the television for some program that was worth watching. He stopped on channel 25, which was transmitting an evangelistic meeting from the city of La Paz, Bolivia. The message caught his interest.

That week I was preaching sermons based on the book of Jonah. This prophet was full of spiritual conflicts. They had left him feeling so confused and rebellious that he couldn't live in peace. When he refused to bring God's warning to the people of Nineveh, God let him go to the bottom of the sea and look death right in the face so he would understand that "salvation is of the LORD" (Jonah 2:9).

At the end of the message, I appealed to the minds and hearts of the audience. I said, "It doesn't matter who you are. You may be a religious leader who is struggling to give yourself completely to Jesus. You may know about religion without knowing Jesus. Religion doesn't transform the heart; Jesus does. And when He does, He changes your whole life as well.

"Tonight I am inviting you to accept Jesus. Leave your preconceptions, your intellectual pride, your diplomas to one side, and come to Jesus as a child. Bring Him your conflicts, your anxieties, your confusions. Let Jesus bring peace to your heart."

Sixto was transfixed. I was describing everything he was feeling. Perhaps, just perhaps, he thought, the trauma he felt in living was due to trusting too much in his mental prowess, in his analytical abilities. That night he understood that he had to come to Jesus as a child would. Suddenly, he found himself on his knees begging for divine mercy.

When Sixto finished praying that night, he felt great peace in his heart. And from that moment on, many things changed in his life—for the better.

*   *   *   *   *

I was in La Serena, a Chilean city bathed by the Pacific Ocean. About two thousand people had come to hear the preaching of God's Word. Right before the sermon, someone told the story of the former Catholic priest who had recently been baptized by immersion in accord with the biblical mandate. He and his wife came to the podium, where he gave a moving testimony. Then they called me over to meet him. He smiled timidly, and I hugged him. There was a lot of emotion in that hug. That man was another trophy of divine love. He was Sixto.

CHAPTER FIVE

Blood Brothers

Noon. The sun shone fiercely, beating down on the bare head of Private Moliner. The young soldier had been standing at attention for three hours, carrying out the punishment imposed on him. Facing a stone wall as the sweat slid down his face, he read over and over an epigraph by Calderón de la Barca that is posted in all the infantry barracks of the army of Spain: "Here the greatest feat is to obey, and it is done by neither questioning nor refusing. Here, more than anywhere else, courtesy, good behavior, the truth, firmness, loyalty, courage, gallantry, credit, opinion, constancy, patience, humility and obedience, fame, honor, and life itself are the fortune of poor soldiers; and in good fortune and bad, the militia is no less than the religion of honorable men."

That is how Javier Moliner Tello became a hard, disciplined soldier. It is how he came to personify the principles of military life. And it's how he became a sergeant and why he was given the job of instructing and disciplining draftees.

Sergeant Moliner had the reputation of being tough—and he was. He was implacable with the undisciplined, hard on the timid, and intransigent with loafers. The inductees trembled in his presence. And sometimes Sergeant Moliner overdid his enthusiasm for military life. On one occasion, he was charged with abuse of authority—he had beaten an inductee who wasn't meeting his standards. Despite this, his superiors kept him at the post of training the new inductees. In their opinion, no one did a better job of turning out courageous, intrepid soldiers than he did.

Spain, where this story took place, requires one year of military service from the life of each of its male citizens. When the crop of new inductees arrived, Sergeant Moliner would order his corporals to "train these men. And," he would add, "if anyone makes trouble that you can't handle, just bring him to me."

Moliner himself had taught these corporals, so they were nearly as ferocious as he was. No trainee was foolish enough to disobey them. They wouldn't take any of their trainees to the sergeant anyway—that would have meant admitting they had failed.

So it was a surprise when one day one of the corporals approached the sergeant with a case that was totally unheard of. The trainee explained the problem. "Sergeant, sir," he said, standing at attention, "I am a Christian, and I must rest on the Sabbath day. In the fourth commandment, God has ordered me to do so."

Sergeant Moliner was an atheist. He had never read the Bible, much less heard of the Sabbath. The only religion he knew was the one de la Barca had written about: "The militia is no less than the religion of honorable men." He couldn't understand how anyone would dare to give an order to one of his soldiers without consulting him.

"Do you know where you are, soldier?" he barked. "This is

the army. It isn't a convent. Here you don't talk about God. Here you obey. And I'm the only one who can give you orders."

"But Sergeant, sir—"

"Leave!"

"Excuse me, sir—"

"Did you hear me, soldier? Leave!"

The soldier, Martínez, withdrew.

Some time later, the sergeant received a letter in which the pastor of Martínez's church advocated his right to rest on the Sabbath. It was, he said, a matter of conscience.

The sergeant already had on his record the incident of his abuse of authority, and he didn't want another offense. So he took the letter to the captain of the company. Two hours later the captain called him and said, "Sergeant, the soldier is right. According to article fourteen of the Spanish Constitution, no one can be discriminated against due to gender, race, or religion."

"Captain, can you imagine what a precedent this situation would set?" Moliner asked. "What will happen to army discipline? Any and every soldier will invent some excuse, and we'll find ourselves obligated to give in."

"I'm sorry, Sergeant, but it's the constitution, and we should be the first to obey it."

Moliner left breathing fire. That little soldier would see more of him! He authorized the trainee's Sabbath rest, but the rest of the week he loosed all his rage against the defenseless man.

The persecution of Private Oscar Martínez was unfair, cruel, and implacable. During the week, in addition to attending the instruction that all the soldiers received, Martínez had to clean the latrines, the weapons room, and the kitchen. And any fault, however small—such as a scuffed boot, hair just a little too long, or a spot on his uniform—was cause for punishment.

And all the soldiers had Sundays off—all except Martínez. Moliner ordered four hours straight of military instruction in the hot sun under four different corporals so that none of them would tire, and he ordered Martínez to clean the bathrooms when the four hours were up. But at the end of the day Martínez presented himself to the sergeant just as he did every time he completed his punishment and said, "Sergeant, I have finished everything, sir. Is there anything else?"

*　*　*　*　*

Every night Moliner came home agitated and irritable. When his wife asked what was wrong, he said angrily, "There's a soldier who is driving me crazy. I don't know what's wrong with him. I impose the worst punishments on him, and he never objects—he just obeys in silence. He even sings while he is carrying out his punishment! I don't know what else to do!"

As the months passed, Sergeant Moliner's rage turned into hatred. The private's humility and submission offended him. He was the superior, but Martínez's attitude made him feel inferior. Worse than that, it made him feel unfair and cowardly.

When he could stand it no longer, he sent for the soldier and asked what enabled him to put up with so many punishments without becoming insubordinate. Martínez looked Sergeant Moliner directly in the eye and responded without blinking. "Sergeant, sir," he said, "Jesus gives me the strength to go on. Nobody likes you, sir, so every day I ask God to change your heart and transform you into a new man."

The words stabbed into Moliner's heart as if they were knives. "Quit speaking such foolishness, soldier!" he roared. Then, pointing at the door, he shouted, "Get out of here!"

"Look for Jesus in Scripture," Martínez said as he left. "The Bible has the answer to all of your problems."

When the door closed behind Martínez, the sergeant was beet red, trembling, and perspiring. He didn't know whether to cry or to scream, to run or to stay still. Private Martínez's words echoed in his mind. Look for Jesus? What did he need from Jesus? The words didn't make sense, but they moved him deeply, hurt him, tormented him. It was so confusing.

That night the sergeant couldn't sleep. His troubled state bothered him so much that he considered going to a psychologist. Having a mere trainee occupy his thoughts so constantly wasn't normal. Why did he bother him so much?

Moliner's wife tried to console him. "Don't worry about it," she told him. "I think you're magnifying the problem."

"But you don't know him, Rosi," he protested, distressed. "It's irritating. It's . . . oh, I don't know how to explain it. Forget it!"

But Moliner himself couldn't forget it. He talked about Martínez all the time. Every evening, Moliner had to tell what he'd done that day.

One sunny Sunday, the sergeant and his wife were strolling hand in hand through a city park. Suddenly, Moliner jolted to a halt and stared. Then, pointing with his finger, he murmured, "There he is, Rosi. There's the soldier who is driving me crazy."

Martínez and his girlfriend were sitting in the grass, chatting animatedly. They hadn't noticed the sergeant.

"Private Martínez!" The sergeant's voice was like thunder. And quick as lightning, the soldier jumped to his feet and saluted.

"Look, Rosi. This is the soldier I told you about."

The soldier, embarrassed, almost begged. "No, please, Sergeant," he said. "I'm with my girlfriend."

Moliner said, "Let's go and get some dinner."

Martínez replied, "Thank you, sir, but we were just leaving."

"I said, 'Let's go and get some dinner'—and don't argue!"

"As you order, sir," the soldier replied, still at attention.

They went to a restaurant nearby, and Sergeant Moliner ordered shrimp and wine for all four.

"Sergeant, sir, you know that I don't eat shrimp nor drink any kind of alcohol."

Moliner looked at his wife and said, "See, Rosi. You said I was exaggerating, but he's like this all the time."

* * * * *

In this life all things eventually end—good times and bad times, happiness and pain. So, that terrible year came to a close at last for Private Martínez. When he had fulfilled his military obligation, he left the army.

Three more years passed. Then, one day while Sergeant Moliner and his wife were vacationing near the port of Sagunto, they were invited to dine with some friends. In the group was a couple who were Christians. This couple asked for permission to thank God for the food before the group started eating.

The couple's request immediately raised in the sergeant's mind the unhappy memory of Private Martínez. He looked at them with apprehension and asked himself, *Are religious fanatics going to pursue me wherever I go? Am I going to keep running into them all my life?*

Halfway through supper, Moliner abruptly burst out, "So do you keep the Sabbath too?"

" 'Too?' Do you know someone else who keeps the Sabbath?"

Moliner regretted having asked. His question had opened the door to a conversation he didn't want—a conversation about spiritual things. To make matters worse, the conversation centered not on the Sabbath but on Christ Jesus.

The couple spoke tenderly each time they mentioned Jesus, and they acted as though Jesus were sitting right there at the table with them. They looked happy, and their happiness didn't seem to be an empty, artificial, external kind. It was a steady joy that bubbled from their souls and was reflected in their eyes, their words, and their attitude. The hard, unbelieving sergeant found it impressive—which was the reason he agreed to study the Bible when someone asked whether he would like to learn more about the divine mysteries.

Moliner and Rosi spent the whole month of August in those Bible studies. Both of them were full of questions. The answers they received were all based on the Bible. Their instructor didn't say what he thought but, rather, what was written in God's Word. That pleased the anxious military man and his wife.

One day Moliner told their instructor, "I don't understand what you're trying to say. If we are saved only by the wonderful grace of Jesus, why is it necessary to keep the commandments?"

Many sincere people had asked the instructor that question before. "Look," he responded, "salvation has two aspects: cause and effect. Obedience to the commandments is not the cause of salvation. The cause of salvation is grace. We are saved exclusively by the grace of God—not because of works or obedience; only because of what Jesus did on the cross at Calvary. But when we are saved, results should follow. We should live like people who have been saved. Jesus said, 'If you love Me, keep My commandments' [John 14:15].

"We don't obey in order to obtain salvation. Obedience is only an expression of the love we feel toward Jesus and evidence that we know Him. 'By this we know that we know Him, if we keep His commandments. He who says, "I know Him," and does not keep His commandments, is a liar, and the truth is not in him. . . . He who says he abides in Him ought himself also to walk just as He walked' " (1 John 2:3, 4, 6).

"So, does being a Christian mean walking as Jesus walked?"

"Exactly, and also doing everything that Jesus did."

"Did Jesus keep the Sabbath?"

"Yes, definitely. Look at this verse: 'So He came to Nazareth, where He had been brought up. And as His custom was, He went into the synagogue on the Sabbath day, and stood up to read' [Luke 4:16].

"Notice that the text says 'as His custom was.' Going to the synagogue on the Sabbath wasn't something He did sporadically. Rather, it was what He always did.

"When Jesus came to this earth, He said, ' "Do not think that I came to destroy the Law or the Prophets. I did not come to destroy but to fulfill. For assuredly, I say to you, till heaven and earth pass away, one jot or one tittle will by no means pass from the law till all is fulfilled" ' " (Matthew 5:17, 18).

Moliner was confused. Lately he had been reading the Bible avidly, and he was finding it difficult to process all the information he was receiving. So, he kept asking questions. "The text that you just read says that Jesus went into the synagogue on the 'Sabbath day,' but it doesn't say Saturday."

"That's right, it doesn't say Saturday. In order to know what day is the true Sabbath, we need to look for an answer in the Bible itself. When Moses was telling the story of Creation, he said, 'Thus the heavens and the earth, and all the host of them, were finished. And on the seventh day God ended His work which He had done, and He rested on the seventh day from all His work which He had done. Then God blessed the seventh day and sanctified it, because in it He rested from all His work which God had created and made' [Genesis 2:1–3].

"Do you see that the day God rested, blessed, and sanctified was the seventh day? Now, tell me, which is the seventh day?"

"Saturday," Moliner responded quickly. Then he immediately asked, "The other day I met a person who said that Saturday was the Sabbath only for the Jews. How true is that?"

"We just read," the instructor replied, "that the Sabbath was established at Creation. At that time there were no Jews. God had just created the first two human beings. And Jesus Himself said, ' "The Sabbath was made for man, and not man for the Sabbath" ' [Mark 2:27]. Notice that Mark says 'man' and not 'Jew.' The Sabbath was established as a blessing for all humanity, not just for the Jews."

"But how can it become a blessing?"

"I'll let the prophet Isaiah answer that."

"If you turn away your foot from the Sabbath,
From doing your pleasure on My holy day,
And call the Sabbath a delight,
The holy day of the LORD honorable,
And shall honor Him, not doing your own ways,
Nor finding your own pleasure,
Nor speaking your own words,
Then you shall delight yourself in the LORD;
And I will cause you to ride upon the high hills of the
      earth,
And feed you with the heritage of Jacob your father.
The mouth of the LORD has spoken" (Isaiah 58:13, 14).

"Do you see what kind of blessings God promises if you obey Him?"

Moliner said, "I want to ask just one more question."

"Ask as many questions as you like. The Bible has the answer to everything we wonder about."

"Wasn't the Sabbath abolished when Jesus died? Didn't He fulfill the law in our place?"

"Let's take a look at what Luke says about Christ's death. 'That day was the Preparation, and the Sabbath drew near. And the women who had come with Him from Galilee followed after, and they observed the tomb and how His body was laid. Then they returned and prepared spices and fragrant oils. And they rested on the Sabbath according to the commandment' [Luke 23:54–56].

"There are two expressions here that I want you to notice. The first is 'they rested on the Sabbath day.' Notice that Jesus was already dead, but the women who followed Him 'rested on the Sabbath day' after His death. That means the Sabbath was still a day of rest.

"The second expression is 'according to the commandment.' What commandment? The fourth commandment of God's law:

> "Remember the Sabbath day, to keep it holy.
> Six days you shall labor and do all your work,
> but the seventh day is the Sabbath of the LORD
> your God. In it you shall do no work: you, nor
> your son, nor your daughter, nor your male ser-
> vant, nor your female servant, nor your cattle,
> nor your stranger who is within your gates.
> For in six days the LORD made the heavens and
> the earth, the sea, and all that is in them, and

rested the seventh day. Therefore the LORD blessed the Sabbath day and hallowed it" [Exodus 20:8–11].

"Oh, and please don't tell me that the law doesn't apply to Christians, because David said, 'The works of his hand are verity and judgment; all his commandments are sure. They stand fast for ever and ever, and are done in truth and uprightness' [Psalm 111:7, 8, KJV]. Every time someone tells you that the law was nailed to the cross and no longer applies to Christians, remember what David said—God's commandments stand fast for ever and ever."

"Does that mean that the law still applies to Christians?" Moliner asked, wide-eyed and anxious.

"Let's look at what Paul wrote," the instructor responded. " 'Do we then make void the law through faith? Certainly not! On the contrary, we establish the law' [Romans 3:31]. You can see that in the life of every authentic Christian there is a place for faith and for law. They don't conflict with each other. Faith is the instrument through which we take hold of Christ's grace, and the law is the path that the Christian travels."

During that month of vacation in Sagunto, Sergeant Moliner saw a fascinating world of fullness and satisfaction in Christ. But what he saw also brought many conflicting feelings. On one hand, he was happy to learn biblical truths that gave meaning to his life. On the other hand, he was filled with remorse because now he understood Private Martínez. The apparent rebellion of the soldier finally started fitting into the complicated puzzle with which the sergeant was struggling. *How could I have done all those terrible things to a young man who just wanted to be faithful to God and his own principles?* he asked himself. His chest tightened, and he fought to restrain the rebellious tears that threatened to flow.

* * * * *

When Sergeant Moliner's vacation ended, he went back to the barracks. However, nothing in the military life he had loved seemed to have meaning anymore. Now he wanted only to study the Bible and to learn more about Jesus. He begged God not to desert him but to be active in his life.

The first day Moliner was back at the base, one of the corporals ran to meet him. The corporal exclaimed, "Sergeant, sir, I have interesting news for you. A new group of inductees just arrived, and among them is one of those Sabbath guys you like so much!"

Moliner felt a chill course through his body. Jesus had answered his prayer!

Sergeant Moliner called for the new inductee to be brought before him. Private Javier Ortega entered Moliner's office trembling. He had heard all about the sergeant. People had told him everything that Martínez had suffered at his hands. "I doubt you'll survive," one of the corporals had said. "The sergeant is going to finish you off!"

The young soldier stood at attention before the fearsome Sergeant Moliner.

"Private Ortega?"

"Yes, sir."

"Sit down and begin telling me about Jesus."

At first Ortega thought that the sergeant was planning to torture him with sarcasm. Then, however, he noticed that the sergeant was looking at him kindly, almost tenderly. The sergeant was sincere. "Three years ago," he told Ortega, "another Christian soldier was here. I mistreated him. I humiliated him. But while I was on vacation this year, I found Jesus, and with you, everything is going to be different. I'll give you complete freedom to serve God and be faithful to Him. I will do for you what I didn't do for Martínez."

74

* * * * *

Months passed during which Sergeant Moliner continued studying the Bible. Eventually, he wanted to be baptized, as did his wife and daughter. And Moliner wanted Martínez, his former trainee, to be present at his baptism. However, he couldn't find his telephone number. Finally, on the Friday before his baptism, someone gave it to him.

Martínez's year in the army had left deep marks on his mind that he wanted to erase. When he'd been released, he'd tried to forget all the suffering he had endured. He knew nothing of what had been happening to Moliner.

One Friday at about ten in the morning, his telephone rang. When he raised the receiver, someone said, "Private Martínez!" in a familiar voice—one that had given him nightmares. One that he never wanted to hear again. So he kept silent.

At the other end of the line the voice spoke again. "Private Martínez, answer me!"

"Yes, sir, Sergeant." Martínez responded automatically.

"I want you here in Seville tomorrow morning at nine o'clock."

Martínez lived in Vigo, more than seven hundred miles from Seville. "Sergeant, sir," he said, "you know that tomorrow is Saturday. I dedicate Saturdays to God."

"But I'm ordering you to come!"

"I am very sorry, sir."

"Then would you accept if I invited you?"

"I can't do it, sir—you know that. Please don't insist."

"Private Martínez," the sergeant said in a voice shaking with emotion, "if I had found your telephone number earlier, I would have called you sooner. But I got it just today. I'm begging you, please come. Tomorrow I will be baptized into the same church you are a member of. You have no idea how much it would mean to me if you would come."

Martínez couldn't believe his ears. He thought the sergeant fully capable of pulling a trick like this just to torment him. He answered, "I'm very sorry, sir, but I don't believe a word you're saying."

"What can I say to make you believe me? I know you have every reason to hate me and not to believe me, but I want you to know that I have accepted Jesus as my Savior. You and your endurance of the pain and humiliation that I caused you were the instruments God used to reach me."

At the other end of the line Martínez was shaking. All the persecution he had suffered paraded through his mind. But something in his heart told him that the sergeant was telling the truth.

"Do you believe me, Martínez?"

The question brought him back to the present. "I believe you, Sergeant, sir."

"Don't call me 'Sergeant.' Call me 'Brother.' Now we are brothers."

Martínez caught the train that afternoon. And the next morning, Moliner anxiously awaited his former soldier at the station in Seville.

The train came into the station at 7:45 A.M., and a crowd of people got off. Moliner searched the throng anxiously. His heart was beating furiously, his throat was tightening, his hands were trembling, and his legs could barely hold him up, such was the load of emotion that he bore. Suddenly he saw him. The same peaceful face, the same deliberate walk, the same understanding expression. When their eyes met, both of them ran forward, embraced, and cried. The persecuted and the persecutor. The sergeant and the private. Now they were blood brothers. Jesus' precious blood had broken down the barriers and built a bridge.

*   *   *   *   *

I was in Madrid holding an evangelistic series. One of the pastors offered to give my wife and me a tour of the Spanish capital. After he showed us the most important places in the ancient city, we drove to the outskirts for lunch.

As we were traveling, the pastor, deeply emotional, told us the story of the miracle. He was the main character in the story. He was the coal snatched from the fire. He was ex-sergeant Moliner.

CHAPTER SIX

The Scapegoat

The news appeared in all the media: "Scandal in the Copper Business." "National Copper Industry Loses 500 Million." "Who Made Off With the 500 Million?" "Earthquake: 300 Million Disappears." It was a bombshell. The gossip of the day in offices, restaurants, and even on street corners. Indignant people speculated about how anyone could get away with five hundred million dollars, though later, the figure became four hundred million, and it ended up being "only" two hundred million. Journalism lives on such news—the more unprecedented and incredible the event, the better the story sells.

The Golden Youth, as Juan Pablo was called, was the stock-broker who negotiated copper sales from his country to the whole world. For years, his mental acuity and business sense had earned millions for the state company he represented. He was considered a financial wizard, and his bosses practically worshiped him. But then one day business went bad. Where there had been profits, there now were losses. So, they started blaming it all on him. Someone had to take the fall, so they made him the scapegoat.

Sitting at a bar in a Paris hotel, Juan Pablo saw the dream castle he had built over the years disintegrate. He knew that if he went home, he would be arrested. He was the key person in the business, but his position was the weakest politically. He knew his name was mud. Those are the breaks in business. One either wins or loses; one defeats others or is defeated by them.

The rumor spread that he had the money hidden away in some foreign country. If that had been true, he would never have returned home. If he'd had millions of dollars, he could easily have fled just about anywhere on earth and lived anonymously but well.

Besides, while Juan Pablo wasn't religious, he had principles. As a child, he had considered himself a Catholic; he was christened and received First Communion. When he grew older, he forgot all that, but the principles he had learned still governed his life. Among them were these codes of conduct: Take responsibility. Never run away. The worst defeat is the battle that is never fought.

So Juan Pablo wouldn't run. Instead, he would fly home to face the storm that awaited him.

The press had pictured him as a skilled swindler who had pocketed millions of dollars, and millions of his fellow citizens now hated him. So the hand of the law came down heavily on him. Accused of tax evasion, he was sentenced to thirty years in prison. He lost everything he possessed and suffered the pain of seeing his family humiliated. The man who had traveled the world, staying in the best hotels and eating at the finest restaurants, now shared a humble cell with five other prisoners.

Sometimes God lets us reach rock bottom in order to remind us that we are not our own—we belong to the God who created us. Jonah recognized that fact while inside the belly of a gigantic fish in the depths of the sea. Saul of Tarsus recognized it in the dust of the desert road to Damascus. Nebuchadnezzar, emperor and builder of mighty Babylon, opened his eyes and heart to God when he was reduced to grazing alongside the beasts of the field and sleeping with them under the trees.

During Juan Pablo's time in prison, he reviewed his life carefully. He realized that he had allowed the bright lights of human glory, the fascination of power, and the enchantment of money to displace God. Now, in the midst of pain and shame, he had no other resource than the Creator.

* * * * *

While Juan Pablo was in prison, many sincere Christians visited him. They tried to convince him to join one church or another. That made him very uncomfortable. He felt as though he were some kind of trophy everyone was fighting over.

Then one dark day in his dark life a very simple man approached him. The man was wearing black pants and a white shirt and looked to be about fifty years old. And though time had creased his face, his eyes were clear, and he seemed to have an aura of peace.

The man came right to the point. "I would like to study the Bible with you," he said. His voice sounded like a quietly flowing brook.

"What church are you from?" Juan Pablo asked, ready to reject him.

"I don't want to talk about churches," the visitor responded. "I just want to talk about Jesus."

"Yes, but in the end you're going to try to get me into your church."

"No, I just want to study the Bible with you."

"What for? What good does it do you to study the Bible with me if you don't want me to join your church?"

"Look, I know who you are. I know you are suffering, and I want to help you."

"How is that Book going to help me?"

"In this Book, God teaches us how to live and how to find the path to true happiness."

"Can anyone be happy in prison?"

"You may not understand it now, but if you study the Bible, you will discover that while people can put your body in prison, they can never imprison your spirit."

"Hmmm, that sounds interesting. What's your name?"

"Fernando."

That is how Juan Pablo started studying the Bible. He brought to his study a very bright, rational brain that held no prejudices. And he was careful. While he didn't want to reject what was good, he didn't want to be so gullible as to believe everything people told him either.

Fernando came to visit every week. Soon Juan Pablo understood the essence of the gospel. Since the fall of our first parents, all human beings have been born with a tendency to distance themselves from God. They want to live alone, independently, doing whatever they want and seeking solely their own gain. Many times this natural stubbornness results in people hurting themselves and those whom they love the most.

By nature, human beings are predisposed to evil. They're naturally selfish. And though they know their behavior will result in destruction, they heedlessly continue it anyway. They can't change their path themselves—to change, they need strength that is superior to their own. They need God. People experience real living only when they become tired of struggling and suffering on their own and they turn to God.

So, a few months after Juan Pablo began to study the Bible, he gave his life to Jesus and experienced a complete turn around spiritually.

* * * * *

Some time later when Fernando came to visit, Juan Pablo began to bombard him with questions. "I can't find a single verse in the Bible that says God changed the day of worship from Saturday to Sunday. Who made that change? Why don't Christians keep Saturday?" he asked anxiously.

Fernando gave him a fatherly glance and said, "It's a long story. I'll begin with a biblical text. God has said,

"My covenant I will not break,
Nor alter the word that has gone out of My lips"
[Psalm 89:34].

"God made a covenant with His people. They would receive His blessing as long as they obeyed His commandments. His people of old failed, but God didn't change. He said He wouldn't alter the word that has gone out of His lips. That promise is still valid today."

"Yes, but when did people start keeping Sunday as their day of rest and worship?"

"As early as Old Testament times God was warning His people against worshiping ' "other gods . . . either the sun or moon or any of the host of heaven" ' [Deuteronomy 17:3]. The first day of the week got its name from the sun. Webster's dictionary says that the name comes from the old English word *sunnan-doeg*—*sunne* meaning 'sun' and *doeg*, 'day.' "

"That makes sense," Juan Pablo commented. "The word *Sunday* means 'day of the sun.' But didn't the apostles keep Sunday?"

"No. Acts chapter eighteen, verse four says of the apostle Paul that 'he reasoned in the synagogue every Sabbath, and persuaded both Jews and Greeks.' This was twenty-three years after Christ's resurrection. So, it is evident that the first day of the week didn't replace the Sabbath in the apostles' time. In fact, nowhere does Scripture record the change, so it must have occurred some time later. It wasn't ever authorized in God's Word."

"Well, who made the change then?"

"Daniel prophesied about the person—or institution—behind the change. The prophet wrote,

" 'He shall speak pompous words against the Most
    High,
Shall persecute the saints of the Most High,
And shall intend to change times and law' " [Daniel
    7:25].

"In chapter seven of his book, Daniel announced the appearance of a religious power that would try to change God's law—especially the commandment related to time, which is the fourth commandment, the commandment about the Sabbath. Today, this religious power openly admits to having made the change. It claims to have transferred the day of worship from Saturday to Sunday. But nowhere does the Bible say that God authorized such a change. Human beings did it."

"So, how did the change occur?" Juan Pablo was curious.

"The first Christians faithfully observed the seventh-day Sabbath after Christ's resurrection. Then the Jews revolted against the Romans. The Roman army fought the Jewish rebels. To escape them, the Jews scattered throughout the empire. The Roman authorities found that they could identify the Jewish rebels by their practice of observing the seventh-day Sabbath. However, the Romans confused the Christians, who also worshiped on the seventh day, with the Jewish rebels.

"Sixtus, bishop of Rome, started the change by authorizing Christians to observe Easter on Sunday rather than on the Passover. By doing this, they could avoid giving the impression that they were Jews."

"It was that simple?"

"No, that was just the beginning," Fernando said. "The Romans already considered Sunday a holiday, in honor of the sun. So Roman worshipers who converted to Christianity preferred worshiping God on the same day on which they had worshiped the sun—on Sunday, in other words.

"Around A.D. 155, Justin Martyr wrote, 'On Sunday we have a common assembly of all our members, whether they live in the city or the outlying districts. . . . We hold our common assembly on Sunday because it is the first day of the week, the day on which God . . . created the world, and because on that same day our Savior Jesus Christ rose from the dead.' "

"That's amazing!" Juan Pablo exclaimed.

"The story doesn't end there," Fernando continued. "The next important step was taken in A.D. 200. The bishop of Rome, Victor, tried to encourage observance of the Resurrection Day among those who still weren't celebrating it. He used Sunday observance to gain control of the Christian church."

"Why did the Christian bishops in other places have to obey the bishop in Rome?"

"Rome was the capital of the empire, so its bishop had greater political influence than any other bishop."

"Is that when Sunday keeping became universal?"

"No. As late as A.D. 450, Socrates Scholasticus, an able historian of the Christian church, wrote, 'Almost all the churches throughout the world celebrate the sacred mysteries on the sabbath of every week, yet the Christians of Alexandria and at Rome, on account of some ancient tradition, have ceased to do this.' "

Juan Pablo said, "I suppose this 'ancient tradition' refers to the emphasis Sixtus and Victor gave to Sunday."

"Exactly," his teacher replied. "The Roman Emperor Constantine also had a lot to do with this change. When he converted to Christianity, he enforced Sunday observance because before his conversion he was a sun worshiper. The first law in favor of Sunday was passed during his tenure, in A.D. 321, and the Christian church, led by the bishop of Rome, transferred the sacredness of Sabbath to Sunday at the Council of Laodicea in the middle of the fourth century A.D."

"Why then do Protestants keep Sunday?"

"That I couldn't tell you. Monsignor Segur, a Catholic priest, wrote, 'The observance of Sunday by the Protestants is an homage they pay, in spite of themselves, to the authority of the [Catholic] Church.' "

"Does that mean that the Church of Rome openly assumes responsibility for having changed Sabbath observance?"

"Yes, Catholics have done so in several of their publications. For example, in the *Catholic Mirror*, Cardinal Gibbon wrote, 'The Catholic Church for over one thousand years before the existence of a Protestant, by virtue of her divine mission, changed the day from Saturday to Sunday.' He also stated, 'You may read the Bible from Genesis to Revelation, and you will not find a single line authorizing the sanctification of Sunday.' "

Juan Pablo pondered these facts for a while and then asked, "Can a person be completely sincere and yet be completely deceived?"

"Yes. But Jesus said, ' "If you were blind, you would have no sin; but now you say, 'We see.' Therefore your sin remains" ' [John 9:41]. Jesus is saying here that no one will be judged for having been deceived, but rejecting truth brings condemnation. God wants people to follow the truth when they see it; otherwise, they're rejecting Him."

"But it's hard for people who have believed something their whole life to change their mind," Juan Pablo protested.

"I suppose it is," Fernando replied. "But look what James wrote: 'To him who knows to do good and does not do it, to him it is sin' [James 4:17]. If you know what is right, you have no choice other than obedience."

"But when someone is sincere, doesn't God take that sincerity into account?"

"I'll let the Lord Jesus Himself answer that one:

" 'In vain they worship Me,
Teaching as doctrines the commandments of men.'

"For laying aside the commandment of God, you hold the tradition of men. . . . All too well you reject the commandment of God, that you may keep your tradition' " (Mark 7:7–9).

Juan Pablo was moved. God's Word was clear. It left no room for argument. Another text he had read shone in his mind: " 'We ought to obey God rather than men' " (Acts 5:29).

*　*　*　*　*

A few months after the discussion about the Sabbath, Juan Pablo decided to be baptized. When he was submerged in the water and then lifted from it, he felt that an old stage of his life was being erased forever and that he was being born again into a new existence.

Soon something happened that offered definite proof that he had begun to live by faith. The test of his faith began when he was diagnosed as having cancer, and, after undergoing many medical tests, received a prognosis that he would live only three more years. Juan Pablo knelt on the floor of his cell and cried out like Jonah from the belly of the great fish. "Lord," he said, "I need You now more than ever before. I know that You have forgiven me, that my old life is over, and that I'm a new creature. I don't need any proof of that. But oh, I would like to see the realness of Your power in my time of physical affliction. Touch my life, my body, and take away this plague."

Two months later, the results of a new examination surprised everyone except Juan Pablo. He'd been totally healed.

More years passed. The press attacked Juan Pablo again. This time they argued that his conversion was just an act to make people forget "the millions of dollars that he had pocketed."

Then a famous reporter interviewed him, and the interview was broadcast during prime time via satellite so the whole country could watch. The reporter said, "People claim that you are just acting holy and that you have the lost money stored away somewhere. They say you became a Christian just to fool the authorities. Is that true?"

The cameras focused on Juan Pablo's hands and face to see whether some involuntary expression would give him away. He smiled—not a sarcastic smile, but rather one of peace—and his eyes reflected his internal calm. Then this notorious man responded. "I can do nothing to make people change their minds about me. I only know that Jesus found me and changed my life. Materially speaking, I have lost everything. But I have won something that is priceless: the wonderful love of Jesus."

It was Friday afternoon. In just three hours I was to preach in a university auditorium, and the next day I would travel to Brazil. But I didn't want to miss what I'd had in mind since I first heard the story.

The doors to the prison opened. I was taken inside to the director's office.

"Wait here, please," the commanding officer of the guards told me.

I waited. A few minutes later, he came in.

No one who could see him at that moment would ever have imagined that here before me was someone who at one time had lived a life of power and abandon. They wouldn't have believed that here was the wizard of the stock market, who was in New York one day and Tokyo the next—who signed million-dollar contracts.

The man who appeared before me that afternoon bore on his face the expression of one who has found Jesus. He looked like someone who had suffered affliction and pain but who now has peace. Even from a distance, his soft voice, shy smile, and clear gaze revealed that.

Yes. That man was a coal snatched from the fire by the wonderful grace of Jesus Christ. He was Juan Pablo.

CHAPTER SEVEN

"You Will Not Surely Die"

"You have twenty-four hours to give us the money, or we will kill your husband." The hoarse voice on the telephone sounded threatening.

Submerged in a world of terror and desperation, she wept like a baby. "It's them! They're going to kill him. I know they're going to kill him!" she cried over and over, while her friends and family tried to calm her down.

The previous two days had been filled with terrible suffering. Her husband had disappeared without a trace. Under such circumstances, the threat, ironically, was a relief. At least now she knew what was happening. Her husband, a famous surgeon, had been kidnapped. He was another victim of urban violence.

During the following days, the family, who acted with guidance from the police, fought a psychological war with the kidnappers. A week later the war came to a tragic conclusion: the family paid the ransom, but the surgeon was killed anyway.

For a moment, the news shook the whole city. The media discussed whether the government should legalize the death penalty for cases of extreme cruelty like this one. But as time passed, everything returned to normal. The surgeon's murder became just one more case file.

While most people went on with life as usual, however, Dina didn't. Consumed by grief and rage, she seemed to be failing like a candle flame about to die out. She stopped eating, refused all visitors, and wouldn't talk with or listen to anyone. She spent all her time gazing at a picture of her husband.

One Sunday morning, immersed in depression, Dina concluded that only death would end her pain. She closed the door to her bedroom, switched on her television set, and turned the volume high so no one would hear the shot. As she was loading the revolver, she heard someone on the TV saying in a calm voice, "If you think that death is the only way out of your problems, stop for a moment and listen to what I have to say. The Lord Jesus Christ died for you on the cross of Calvary. You don't need to die; you just need to trust.

"I know that the pain lacerating your heart prevents you from trusting. When you look around, you see only betrayal, violence, and injustice. From a human point of view, it seems as though there's no point to living in this sin-ravaged world. However, there's Someone who understands your pain. You can't see Him or touch Him, but He's close to you, and He's reaching out with open arms, inviting you to come to Him. Rest in His embrace, and cry out all of the poison that is destroying you."

Laying the gun down, Dina fell to her knees and, weeping in agony, poured out before God all her misery. Then, before she finished her prayer, she raised her eyes toward heaven and said, "Who are You, Lord? Reveal Yourself to me. Come into my life, light my way, and teach me how to live."

When Dina left her room, she was a new woman. It was as if she had awakened from a long sleep and could see before her the dawn of a bright new day.

* * * * *

Dina began studying the Bible with a pastor who lived nearby. The pain she had felt stemmed not only from the inner turbulence caused by her beloved husband's cruel death but also from her confusion regarding what had become of him after he died. Dina wanted to understand the mystery of death. Some people said that at death, human beings are destined to go to Paradise, purgatory, or hell and that their behavior during their life on earth determines which destination they enter. Others said that when people die, their body goes into a grave, but their spirit lives on forever, becoming reincarnated in other forms.

As Dina studied the Bible, she was fascinated by the subject of the state of the dead. Her eyes were opened to truths she had never known, and in the light of biblical teachings, all her questions began to disappear.

The pastor who was leading Dina through the Bible said, "In order to understand what happens to people when they die, we first need to understand how they became alive." Then he read from the Bible: " 'The LORD God formed man of the dust of the ground, and breathed into his nostrils the breath of life; and man became a living soul' " (Genesis 2:7, KJV).

"This verse," the pastor continued, "says that human beings are made of two things: 'the dust of the ground' and 'the breath of life.' God formed the first person, Adam, from 'dust.' Before Adam received the breath of life, he had a brain, but he couldn't think. He had a heart, but it didn't beat. He had muscles, but he couldn't move. And he had lungs, but he couldn't breathe. Then God breathed into his nostrils the breath of life, and what was the result?"

"Adam became a living soul," Dina answered.

"Exactly!" the pastor affirmed. "When you connect a light-bulb to an electric current, light results. If you disconnect the bulb from the electricity, the light no longer exists. Similarly, when a body made from dust receives the breath of life—which comes only from God—life results. When they are separated, the life no longer exists."

"So, what happens when a person dies? What happened to my husband?" Dina asked anxiously.

"I'll let the Bible answer you," the pastor replied.

> Then the dust will return to the earth as it was,
> And the spirit will return to God who gave it
> (Ecclesiastes 12:7).

"In this verse Solomon declared that when people die, their bodies return to the earth. That confirms what God had already said. He told Adam that eventually, he would

> "return to the ground,
> For out of it you were taken;
> For dust you are,
> And to dust you shall return" (Genesis 3:19).

"Pastor," Dina interrupted, "I have no doubt about what happens to the body after death. We all know the corpse is taken to the cemetery and after a few years there is nothing left but dust. The problem isn't the body but rather the spirit. Where does the spirit go?"

"Well, in the verse in Ecclesiastes, Solomon stated that the 'spirit'—or in other words, the breath of life—'will return to God who gave it.' So there is no thinking spirit. Remember that we already saw that a man who could think was produced only when the body, made of dust, was joined with the breath of life. Separated, neither the dust nor the breath of life thinks or feels. Life ends—it no longer exists—when these two components are separated.

"Here's what Solomon said about it in another place:

> The living know that they will die;
> *But the dead know nothing,*
> And they have no more reward,
> For the memory of them is forgotten.
> Also their love, their hatred, and their envy have now
>   perished;
> Nevermore will they have a share
> In anything done under the sun (Ecclesiastes 9:5, 6;
>   emphasis added).

"Does that mean my husband isn't suffering or happy or feeling anything else?"

"That is what the Bible teaches. That's why a few verses on, Solomon wrote, 'Whatever your hand finds to do, do it with your might; for there is no work or device or knowledge or wisdom in the grave where you are going' " (Ecclesiastes 9:10).

Dina was still curious. "Pastor," she said, "I've always heard that the spirit doesn't die but is simply changed—that this life is just a step into other lives. If what you're saying is true, where did this idea come from?"

"That idea has an interesting origin," the pastor answered. "In telling the story of Creation, Moses wrote that God told

Adam he could eat freely of nearly all the trees of the Garden. ' "But of the tree of the knowledge of good and evil you shall not eat, for in the day that you eat of it *you shall surely die*" ' [Genesis 2:17; emphasis added].

"The next chapter says that the devil came along disguised as a serpent and contradicted God's warning: 'The serpent said to the woman, *"You will not surely die"* ' [Genesis 3:4; emphasis added]. His words comprise the first lie recorded in the Bible.

"Eve had to choose between believing God and believing the serpent. God had said that if humans disobeyed, they would die; but the enemy declared the contrary: 'You will not surely die.' "

"Does that mean that the spirit isn't immortal?" Dina inquired.

"According to the Bible, it isn't," the pastor replied. "Of the Lord Jesus, Paul wrote that He *'alone has immortality'* [1 Timothy 6:16; emphasis added]. If the Bible declares that God is the only One who is immortal, you can understand that all the people who believe that human spirits keep living after death just don't know their Bible."

"But if people live good lives on this earth, isn't it logical that they will go to heaven when they die?"

The pastor responded, "The Bible says David was a man after God's own heart. But in the sermon Peter preached at the Feast of Pentecost, he declared of David that ' "he is both dead and buried, and his tomb is with us to this day. . . . For David did not ascend into the heavens" ' " (Acts 2:29, 34).

"Pastor," Dina exclaimed wonderingly, "the Bible is clear! God considered David to be His servant. So if David didn't go to heaven when he died but rather is still in the grave, then I have no doubt human spirits must not return to God."

"Well, Dina, Ecclesiastes chapter twelve, verse seven speaks of the spirit returning to God who gave it. But that verse doesn't say 'the spirit of the good person returns to God.' It makes no distinction between good people and bad ones. So we have to ask ourselves what the word *spirit* means in this verse.

"The Old Testament of the Bible was originally written in Hebrew. The Hebrew word behind the English word *spirit* is *ruah,* which may also be translated 'breath' or 'puff.' Nowhere does the Bible imply that this 'breath' or 'puff' or 'spirit' can think or is conscious of anything. David himself said,

The dead do not praise the LORD,
Nor any who go down into silence [Psalm 115:17].

"The Bible never suggests that the spirit is some kind of second life-form that has a continued existence separate from the body. To the contrary, it clearly states that when human beings are dead, they have no consciousness of what happens to them. If the spirit that returns to God were capable of continuing to act when separated from the body, then surely it would praise God when it is in His presence. But David said that the dead do not praise God. Why? Simply because the spirit that returns to God is no more than a breath and isn't conscious of anything."

At this point in the study, Dina felt as though fresh air were blowing through her soul. Peace filled her heart at the assurance that her beloved husband wasn't suffering nor was he worrying about the problems people on this earth were facing.

Though Dina felt at peace, she still felt a sense of loss as well. Would she ever see her husband again?

Carried away by grief and the pain of separation, many people who have lost a loved one turn to spiritualism, which promises to connect them with the spirits of their departed loved ones. Dina now realized that the archenemy of God, who appeared in the Garden of Eden telling the lie that humans wouldn't die, will do everything in his power to foster that same lie in the present day. The apostle Paul declared that the same being who took on the form of a serpent to catch the unguarded attention of Eve and Adam also "transforms himself into an angel of light" (2 Corinthians 11:14). If he disguised himself as a serpent and an angel of light, why wouldn't he disguise himself as the spirit of a dead person as well?

What then can people do about loss and loneliness? What hope is there, and what comfort for people who, like Dina, have been cruelly separated from a loved one? The pastor opened his Bible once more and showed her the answer.

"For a Christian, death is just a sleep. The apostle John recorded a revealing interchange between Jesus and His disciples. Some time after Jesus heard that Lazarus, a follower of His, was sick, He said, ' "Our friend Lazarus sleeps, but I go that I may wake him up." Then His disciples said, "Lord, if he sleeps he will get well." However, Jesus spoke of his death, but they thought that He was speaking about taking rest in sleep. Then Jesus said to them plainly, "Lazarus is dead" ' [John 11:11–14].

"We can see here that Jesus called Lazarus's death 'sleep.' That isn't unusual. Death is compared to sleep in more than fifty places in the Bible. For example, David prayed,

> Consider and hear me, O LORD my God;
> Enlighten mine eyes,

Lest I *sleep the sleep of death* [Psalm 13:3; emphasis
added].

"Death is like a sleep. Why do we not fear going to sleep?
Because we know that we will wake up the next morning. In
light of that, think about this divine promise: ' "The hour is
coming in which all who are in the graves will hear His voice
and come forth" ' [John 5:28, 29].

"The resurrection, which Jesus was talking about in this
verse, is the divine answer to the problem of death. It is the
solution for the suffering caused by that loss—for the anguish
of separation. The apostle Paul confirmed this promise. To the
Christians in Thessalonica he wrote, 'I do not want you to be
ignorant, brethren, concerning those who have fallen asleep,
lest you sorrow as others who have no hope. For if we believe
that Jesus died and rose again, even so God will bring with Him
those who sleep in Jesus. . . . For the Lord Himself will descend
from heaven with a shout, with the voice of an archangel, and
with the trumpet of God. And the dead in Christ will rise first' "
(1 Thessalonians 4:13, 14, 16).

This biblical passage completed the picture in Dina's mind.
Now everything was clear. There were no more doubts. The Bible
explained away all the mystery of death. There was no reason to
be depressed and anxious, asking herself every day where her beloved husband was, thinking that she had lost him forever. Paul's
promise was clear: don't sorrow like others who have no hope.

At the death of a loved one, those who have no hope may go
crazy, sink into depression, and even try to commit suicide.
Those who have hope react differently. They may cry and feel
sad because of the separation, but they are encouraged by the
certainty that Jesus will return and their loved ones will awake
from the sleep of death to live forever.

When the rainy season came and life began bursting forth in flowers and blades of grass, Dina felt that her life was awakening as well. She had never before felt such a desire to live. The Bible had answered many of the questions that had always bothered her. Now life had meaning. She knew where she had come from and where she was going, and she decided to be baptized, following Jesus' commandment and example.

* * * * *

The brutal cold of winter in Curitiba, Brazil, was beginning to wane. The sun was shining with greater intensity, announcing the coming of a spring full of life. Sandra took off her coat and sat down on the lawn of the university where she was a student. However, her sad gaze didn't match the exuberance of the day. Her heart still bled every time she remembered the cruel death of her father. She had loved him so much, and his absence hurt terribly. But what hurt even more was knowing that her mother, Dina, hadn't managed to overcome the trauma—had instead sunk into a dark world of depression.

"How's my pretty kitty?" The voice startled her out of her thoughts. Henry was a classmate and a good friend.

"I'm surviving," Sandra answered slowly, discouragedly— almost as if she spoke out of obligation rather than friendship.

"I have an invitation for you. Tonight, in the Crystal Palace, there's going to be a seminar on the mystery of suffering. I want you to go with me. I'm sure it would do you a lot of good."

Sandra wasn't sure she wanted to go. So many questions hounded her. If there really was a God of love and if He really did care about His children, why hadn't He done anything to save her father from the kidnappers? Her father had been a good man. As a surgeon, he had saved many lives. He didn't deserve such a cruel death. Sandra longed to understand the mystery of suffering, so she decided to accept the invitation.

When the program started, the music touched Sandra's heart. It spoke of hope, of safety, of victory despite the difficulties of life. And the first thing the evangelist did when he walked to the podium was to open his Bible. "You didn't come to listen to my words," he said. "I'm certain that all of you want to hear God's words, so let's open the Scripture."

That attitude impressed Sandra. Since her father's death, she had heard so much from so many people. All those people were attempting to bring her comfort, but nothing they said healed the terrible wound in her heart.

The evangelist read a passage from Psalms:

God is our refuge and strength,
A very present help in trouble (Psalm 46:1).

Then he said, "Listen closely to God's promise here. He isn't promising that in this world you will never have trouble. What the Lord assures you is that in the midst of those troubles, He will be your refuge, your strength, your help.

"Oh, my friend, at this very moment you may be struggling in the valley of pain and death. You may feel that your strength is exhausted, and you can't stand anymore. The weight of suffering may be so heavy that you feel like your heart is going to explode. But in the name of Jesus I beg you to go to Him. Bring Him your pain and your tears. Bring Him the sadness of your heart. Hide in His arms. Don't leave here tonight without giving your life to Jesus."

At the close of his sermon, the evangelist asked all those who wanted to give their lives to Jesus to come to the front of the auditorium for a special prayer. While people made their way forward, a young woman sang of the pain we suffer because of the evil in this world and of our struggle to understand. Her song spoke of how sometimes it is pain that enables us to touch the hand of God. It ended with the promise that one day grief will end and Jesus will dry all our tears.

That song touched Sandra's heart and made her weep. She decided that she too wanted to give her life to Jesus, so she stood up and went forward. She felt as though the preacher's prayer was her prayer, and her tears washed away the pain that had been suffocating her. When she returned to her dorm that night, she fell asleep with a feeling of peace in her heart for the first time since the tragedy.

* * * * *

December arrived, and Campo Grande, where Dina lived, was dressed in many colors. Christmas music could be heard everywhere. Stores attracted customers with tempting offers. For many of them December meant presents—toys and goodies—and that was all.

Not for Dina. So many things had happened during the past year: the death of her husband; the terrible, dark period of depression; the lamentable moment when she almost took her life; her miraculous encounter with Jesus; and her discovery of Bible truth. Now all that remained was for her to be baptized.

But Dina was afraid. She feared how Sandra, her daughter, would react when she heard that Dina was being baptized. Sandra lived in Curitiba, six hundred miles from Campo Grande. They called each other frequently, but neither had ever mentioned what was happening in her life.

Sandra had loved her father deeply, and Dina knew that although he had died, Sandra continued to respect the customs he had left as a legacy for his family. Dina thought that if she told

Sandra she was planning to be baptized, Sandra would think she was betraying the memory of her husband. She knew her daughter had also been suffering terribly since the death of her father, and she didn't want to upset her.

However, Dina didn't want to start the new year without being born again through baptism. Yet she felt she couldn't be baptized without telling her daughter about this important decision. So, after praying a lot, Dina gathered her courage and called her.

"Sandra, dear, it's me—your mother."

Sandra always enjoyed hearing her mother's voice. The young college student had been very worried about her mother. She knew she had been going through a period of terrible depression.

"Mom! Hi! How are you?"

"I'm fine, dear. I'm calling about something very important, and I want to count on your understanding."

"Of course, Mom. What is it?"

"First, I want you to promise me that no matter what I say, you will try to understand and accept my decision."

"Mom, you're scaring me. What's going on?"

"Nothing, my dear. Just promise me that you'll be understanding."

Sandra thought her mother must have discovered that she had accepted Jesus, received Bible studies, and was ready to be baptized. She hadn't wanted to say anything to her mother because she was afraid of how Dina would react. Now it appeared that her mother had discovered everything.

"Mother dear," Sandra said hesitantly, "forgive me. I was going to tell you, but I just didn't know how."

"What are you talking about, dear?"

"Oh, Mom, listen to me, please! I don't want to hurt you, and I don't want to betray Daddy's memory. But quite some time ago I went to a seminar by Pastor Bullón. I gave my life to Jesus and decided to be baptized. I don't know how you feel about that—I only want you to know that I love you very much, and I hope that even if you can't understand, you will trust me."

On the other end of the line, Dina had begun to cry. That frightened Sandra. "Mommy," she said, "please forgive me, I beg you. I didn't want to hurt you."

Dina cried for a while longer but eventually managed to calm herself. Then she said, "Sandra, dear, I'm not upset—I'm happy! At the worst moment of my life, I heard Pastor Bullón preaching on television, and I, too, gave my life to Jesus and decided to be baptized!"

Sandra couldn't believe her ears. She didn't know whether what she was hearing was true or whether she was dreaming. In His grace, God had mysteriously, wonderfully, led both of them. The next day, Dina, in Campo Grande, and Sandra, in Curitiba, went into the baptismal waters to seal their pact of love with Christ.

* * * * *

Thousands of people were participating in a congress in the mountains of Atibaia, near São Paulo. A pastor pointed and told me, "There she is."

During a break in the meetings, I went over. She recognized me and hugged me. There was a lot of emotion in that greeting. Her eyes shone. All the signs of suffering had disappeared from her face. Her countenance radiated the peace of a woman who has met Jesus and given her life to Him. She was conclusive proof that God's love can work wonders in the life of those who seek Him sincerely. She was Dina.

CHAPTER EIGHT

"If I Were Hungry, I Would Not Tell You"

The sun was dying on the horizon, and Elco was hungry. The food had run out two weeks before, and he'd been surviving on cactus and roots. He was tired of eating cactus.

Elco looked at his watch. It was six o'clock in the evening. He'd been working since six o'clock that morning. The boss might show up that day, and he must have the work done if he hoped to get any pay. He needed money to get out of that place—he couldn't stand the thought staying there any longer. But the closest town—Bronco, New Mexico—was sixty-two miles away.

While he was sitting on a huge boulder and watching the ground squirrels—field rats—he had an absurd idea. He'd actually picked up a rock, but then he'd tried to get the idea out of his head. However, hunger hurts. Eat rats? The suggestion would have seemed absurd to anyone who had anything else to eat, but to Elco it didn't seem senseless. Sometimes survival is all that matters.

False promises had lured Elco and four other people to this ranch. For undocumented workers like themselves, the salary seemed attractive. But the reality was cruel. The place was semidesert—hot during the day and cold at night. When the wind blew during the dark hours, it sounded like the howling of hungry wolves. The boss appeared only sporadically, and the food he brought didn't last long. Most days the workers were hungry. They had to invent means of survival.

Lying on his narrow cot that night, Elco tried unsuccessfully to sleep. His life seemed so empty that he felt like crying. He had struggled with all his strength and will since he left Chihuahua, his home state in Mexico. But it was all for naught. The American dream seemed less and less attainable. It had become the American nightmare.

"Men never cry," Elco's grandfather had told him when he was a child. Now he was a strong man who wasn't afraid of anything. But that night he felt like crying—and he did cry. But Elco's tears were not born of fear or hunger or even loneliness. They were born of rebellion. He couldn't accept his circumstances. He needed to get away. This new country meant only failure. He had failed—but he wasn't about to give up. He was Elco Marquez, a true-blue Mexican, and Mexicans never give up. Tomorrow would be another day.

* * * * *

Dallas. Atlanta. Washington, D.C., Elco devoured the miles, running like a pursued man. He worked as much as sixteen hours a day, searching for a better tomorrow. At first he thought he was searching for money—there was never enough money. Later, he decided money could never fill the void in his heart.

Once, in Dallas again, he sensed danger in the darkness of the street. Three men were following him—he could hear their footsteps and see their shadows. He knew they were going to rob him. He had sixty dollars—money earned by the sweat of his brow. It wasn't fair that they were going to take it. But who cared whether life was fair for him? Those men didn't. They stabbed him in the back and left him bleeding and needing help. However, he didn't have any papers—he was an illegal immigrant—and he feared the authorities would send him back to Mexico. So he coped on his own. He wasn't about to give up—to return to his country as poor as he came would be to retreat from the battlefield. He had come to conquer, and conquer he would.

Elco kept on running. Years passed, and he saw more cities, jobs, and people. Then one day he met Margarita. Her dark skin and black eyes enchanted him. Every time he saw her, his heart pounded, his hands sweated, and his words got all tangled up. Paradoxically, she also filled him with peace. She was an oasis in his tormented life.

They were married in Chihuahua, her home state as well as his. Returning home was exciting. That's where he had played as a boy. It's where he'd dreamed and cried and laughed—and where at sixteen he'd ridden broncos. Like life itself, the colts were rebellious, untamable. That's what made him a fighter, untiring.

But those qualities seemed to be of no use to him. He was still poor. His work made his bosses rich, but his own pockets were still empty—just like his heart. This race had no end. He was still searching, searching, searching.

Soon Elco and Margarita were expecting a baby. They tried Baltimore then, but they still couldn't find enough work. When the baby was born, they had no money for milk and diapers. They were drowning in debt—and anxiety. Elco decided that they had to move again, to search somewhere else.

Florida, their next stop, changed their lives forever. There, fortune finally began to smile on them. Elco and two partners opened a construction business. It kept them busy and fed, clothed, and housed them.

Then one day Elco discovered the business was nearly a million dollars in the red. That sank him into despair. Humanly speaking, there was no way out. Many people die without ever seeing that much money. Where had it gone? Why had they never noticed what was happening? Why had they let the business get so deep in trouble? Elco felt like a wild lion captured and caged with no way of escape. He nearly went crazy, not knowing what to do or where to go. But he refused to give up

Eventually, Elco thought of God. When he was a boy he always went to Mass, but at fourteen he'd put religion aside. In his battle to achieve the American dream, he had forgotten God. He had always managed to survive on his own. Now, however, he knew that it was useless to fight. He wished he could vanish or that he could just go to sleep and never wake up, but he had a family. So, instead, he turned to God. "Lord," he prayed, "don't abandon me. Help me find a way out of this pit of debt."

*   *   *   *   *

A series of evangelistic meetings being held in Winter Park, Florida, was being broadcast by satellite for the Hispanic population throughout the United States. Margarita had been going to church. She believed in God with her whole heart, and she knew that only God could work the miracle of getting Elco's business out of debt. So she invited Elco to attend these meetings near their home in Jacksonville, Florida. His feeling of helplessness in the face of his debts made him willing to consider what God had to offer, so he decided one night to go.

The message the evangelist preached the first night that Elco attended fit his life almost as if the speaker knew him personally.

It touched his heart and made him shiver and sweat. But his whole life had been a fight, and he resisted the call to commit himself to God. That night he went home feeling frustrated. He feared that he had let the biggest opportunity of his life get away.

The next day Elco had to go to Savannah, Georgia, on business. As he was driving, he pondered the message he had heard the previous night. He knew that if he gave his heart to Jesus, he must do so completely, and that scared him. He'd heard about tithe—giving one-tenth of one's income to support God's work on earth. But when he thought about the terrible situation his business was in, he knew he couldn't give even one penny to God.

Elco had invited Margarita to make the trip with him. She sat beside him in silence. She had no idea what thoughts were going through his mind, though she knew that something was bothering him. He wasn't his usual self. She knew he'd hardly slept the previous night. That had never happened before. And then he'd invited her along on the ride to Savannah. He had business to do that day, but that was just an excuse. The truth was he needed to talk to her about tithing. He felt that tithe was the great barrier preventing him from committing himself to Jesus.

Elco asked Margarita about tithing. "Why should I give money to God?" he said. "He's God. He doesn't need anything."

Margarita pulled a Bible from the glove compartment of the car and read counsel that the apostle Paul wrote to his protégé Timothy: " 'We brought nothing into this world, and it is certain we can carry nothing out. . . . Those who desire to be rich fall into temptation and a snare, and into many foolish and harmful lusts which drown men in destruction and perdition.

For the love of money is a root of all kinds of evil, for which some have strayed from the faith in their greediness, and pierced themselves through with many sorrows' [1 Timothy 6:7, 9, 10].

"You know, dear," she said, "people who aren't Christian often have a materialistic view of life. They measure success by how much they have. In the text I just read, Paul warned against such values. He declared that we can't take anything with us when we leave this world and that the love of money has led many people to ruin."

Elco was impressed. During the past few weeks the same thought had crossed his mind many times: he had tried to go further than his resources would allow and had gotten into terrible problems. But he still wanted to know why anyone should give money to God.

Margarita read from her Bible again, this time from Psalms.

> The earth is the LORD's and all its fullness,
> The world and those who dwell therein (Psalm 24:1).

> "Every beast of the forest is Mine,
> And the cattle on a thousand hills.
> I know all the birds of the mountains,
> And the wild beasts of the field are Mine.

> "If I were hungry, I would not tell you;
> For the world is Mine, and all its fullness" (Psalm 50:10–12).

She said, "God owns everything; He doesn't need anything. He declares, ' "If I were hungry, I would not tell you." ' "

These psalms only added to Elco's confusion. Then Margarita read,

> "I will rebuke the devourer for your sakes,
> So that he will not destroy the fruit of your ground,
> Nor shall the vine fail to bear fruit for you in the field,"
> Says the LORD of hosts;
> "And all nations will call you blessed,
> "For you will be a delightful land" (Malachi 3:11, 12).

Debt was destroying Elco's business. The harder he worked to pay the people he owed, the further in debt he went. But in the text Margarita read, God promised that He would rebuke the devourer. If He were doing that for Elco, his business would be prospering. But the exact opposite was happening. His business was sterile; it bore only losses. The devourer was destroying everything he had. Elco wondered why this was happening.

Margarita answered his question about the promise by reading the verses that preceded the ones she had just read. Those verses said,

> "Will a man rob God?
> Yet you have robbed Me!
> But you say,
> 'In what way have we robbed You?'
> In tithes and offerings.
> You are cursed with a curse,
> For you have robbed Me,
> Even this whole nation.
> Bring all the tithes into the storehouse,
> That there may be food in My house,
> And prove Me now in this,"

Says the LORD of hosts,
"If I will not open for you the windows of heaven
And pour out for you such blessing
That there will not be room enough to receive it"
    (Malachi 3:8–10).

Elco trembled. Even though he hated to admit it, the truth was crystal clear: in not returning to God a tithe of his income, he had been robbing God. That was the key to the whole thing—the explanation for his constant failures. And what did he have to offer God now? Nothing. Or, more accurately, just debts, desperation, and anxiety.

Interstate 95 extended in front of Elco and Margarita like an endless rope. Thousands of cars were going from here to there and from there to here. The scenery was beautiful, a living landscape painted in nature's own colors. However, none of this drew Elco's attention. He was still thinking. *If God owns everything and has need of nothing, why does He ask human beings to return ten percent of their earnings?* The answer was becoming clear to Elco. The fact that God owns everything, including the goods that come into our hands, isn't theory or philosophy. It is reality. But the only way to make it real in our lives is by returning to God a tenth part of everything He has entrusted to us. Acknowledging this fact in this concrete way—by paying tithe—puts us under divine protection. To deny it is to put ourselves at the mercy of the devourers and destroyers of life.

Now a battle raged inside Elco. His heart was saying, *Trust in the Lord,* but his mind was screaming, *What does God have to do with everything I have earned by my own efforts and determination?*

Margarita interrupted his thoughts with another scriptural passage: " ' "[Beware] when your heart is lifted up, and you forget the LORD your God . . . [and] say in your heart, 'My power and the might of my hand have gained me this wealth.' And you shall remember the LORD your God, for it is He who gives you power to get wealth" ' " (Deuteronomy 8:14, 17, 18).

It is incredible how through the Bible God has provided answers for all the questions of the human heart. Now Elco had no doubt. He knew he needed to make a decision, and it had to be a complete one. He must give Jesus not only his heart but also his body, his business, and his money.

Elco stopped and filled the car with gas. When he pulled out of the gas station, he said, "Let's go back to Jacksonville. I don't want to miss tonight's meeting."

*   *   *   *   *

The trip back to Jacksonville gave Elco time to get a lot of things straight. For him, God had meant no more than a name and the making of the sign of the cross when he passed a church or in times of danger. Spiritually, he had lived alone. He was always busy. He had reserved no time for God.

The message he heard at the meeting the night before was about that. "You came from your Creator's hands," the evangelist said. "You will never be happy until you return to Him. Away from Him you can struggle, run, work—make every effort you want. You may achieve some things, but you will always be unhappy, and you will always feel empty and dissatisfied. You need God. You may not know it but you need Him.

"Come to Jesus tonight. Put your dreams, your plans, your work in His hands, and everything will start to make sense."

Elco's eyes were fixed on the road, but a tear slipped down his cheek. Margarita said nothing. The silence of the man she loved was a temple, and she respected it. She knew that the Holy Spirit was working on his heart. She had been praying a long time for this miracle.

Margarita had already given her heart to Jesus and been baptized, but her happiness was incomplete. Every day she asked God to touch the heart of the father of her children. At first, Elco had been hard. He hadn't wanted to hear anything about the gospel. Later, he had become indifferent, and that wasn't any better. Now, she saw a miracle beginning to happen. Elco was starting to change. He had been thinking about the causes of the disaster his business was facing and had concluded that it was due to the lack of God's presence and blessing in his life.

Jesus said those who are wise—those who hear His words and do them—are like people who build their homes on rock. What they've built can stand the tests that the storms of life bring. The foolish, on the other hand—those who hear His words but don't do them—are like people who build their homes on sand. (See Matthew 7:24–26.)

Build on the rock or build on the sand—that is the great difference between being full and being empty, between hope and despair, between victory and defeat. Building on the rock means recognizing the limits of created beings and accepting God as the beginning, the middle, and the end of our existence. Building on the sand means keeping God out of one's life and pursuing one's own plans. It means searching and not finding, running but never arriving, doing and never accomplishing.

Elco had only two options open to him: rock or sand. He needed to choose.

* * * * *

At eight o'clock that evening, Elco and his wife entered the church. In front, there was a giant screen. The program was starting—transmitting live from Orlando.

Elco had a premonition that this would be a great night. He wanted to catch every detail of the program.

The message seemed to be directed right at him. The preacher read from the book of Matthew: " ' "seek first the kingdom of God and His righteousness, and all these things shall be added to you" ' " (Matthew 6:33).

What things? The verses right before this one have the answer: " 'Do not worry, saying, "What shall we eat?" or "What shall we drink?" or "What shall we wear?" For after all these things the Gentiles seek. For your heavenly Father knows that you need all these things' " (verses 31, 32).

God didn't say that people shouldn't work to supply their needs. He said that if they put their needs first and forget about God, all their efforts will be fruitless. Make God the foundation of your plans and projects, the preacher said. He is the Rock. When you are right with God, everything else will fall into place and make sense.

When the appeal was made, Elco trembled. On the screen, all that could be seen was the preacher's face. Elco lowered his gaze. He felt like the preacher was looking straight at him and knocking on the door of his heart. The Holy Spirit was at work again—the blessed Spirit who never tires of calling us.

Rock or sand. Fullness or emptiness. Where should he go? The preacher called those who wished to give their lives to Jesus to come to the front of the auditorium. Elco resisted no longer. He yielded. He gave himself to Jesus. Crying silently, he stood up and went forward.

*　*　*　*　*

Midnight. Elco was praying. He told God the story of his life, his frustrations and failures. Then he felt the comfort of the Holy Spirit, and indescribable peace filled his heart.

There was still the debt of nearly a million dollars that Elco couldn't pay. On other nights the thought of that debt would have kept him awake. He would have tossed and turned in bed, despairing, trying to find a way out. But that night was different. After Elco prayed, he went to sleep. Angels watched over him while he slept, and other angels began to work at preparing a solution for this man who had given his life to Christ.

The next morning a church member who was in the very last stages of cancer phoned Elco. The man's voice gave the impression that he was fading away, but it also conveyed peace and security. "Elco," the man said, "no matter what happens, everything is going to turn out all right. Just trust God."

The call scared Elco. No one knew the terrible financial situation he was in. How had this man found out? Elco still had a lot to learn about divine mysteries. He was barely a newborn babe in spiritual things.

The first thing Elco did at the end of that week was to take the tithe out of his paycheck. It's easy to *say* that God is the Owner of everything, but *acting* on that statement takes faith. Elco knew what the Bible says, and he chose to enter into the reality of God's promises. It was like stepping out into the dark. That's what Elco did. He put God in first place and trusted that as the Bible promises, God would supply everything he needed.

* * * * *

Monday. A new workweek of challenges and struggles. But Elco was no longer alone. Jesus was at his side. Elco couldn't see Him or touch Him, but he felt Him. He saw Him with the eyes of faith.

Then Elco received a mysterious phone call from an old friend. This friend called to invite him to build a house for a military man. Elco said No. He was scared. His business was in debt, and he didn't have the capital necessary to start such a large project. He thought it would be foolish to sign a contract when he didn't know whether he would be able to fulfill it.

But the friend insisted that Elco take the job, so Elco drove over to talk to him. When he arrived, he found that they had the contract all drawn up, just waiting for his signature. The job would cost several million dollars, and the first payment would completely cover Elco's debt. It was a really good deal, and there was no way it wouldn't work out.

When Elco left, he raised his eyes to heaven and gave thanks. The divine promise was real! No one has ever gone to Jesus sincerely and come away frustrated. If God's promises don't come true, the fault doesn't lie with God. He is perfect, and His promises are perfect as well. It's the human beings who err. They let themselves become trapped in doubts and unbelief, and then they suffer from despair and run through the shadows of their own selfishness without knowing where to go.

Elco had escaped that. He was a new creation now. The sun of a new day shone in his life. He was happy and successful.

* * * * *

Atlanta is a beautiful, majestic city—the home of Martin Luther King Jr. and CNN International. I was preaching in Atlanta, and satellite technology was carrying the message across the whole country. Thousands of people throughout the nation were hearing the good news about Jesus. It is wonderful that the gospel can be spread so easily.

I was sitting in the wings of the stage, watching people rush back and forth when I saw a strong, dark man whose face showed the scars of the hard life he had lived. But he spoke softly, and his eyes reflected the peace of someone who has learned to trust Jesus. He was another divine miracle. He was the man in our story. He was Elco.

CHAPTER NINE

AIDS Countdown

"I am very sorry—you have AIDS."

The doctor's words—to the point, plainly spoken—left Lucía stupefied. She was a successful lawyer—a refined, courteous woman accustomed to dealing with all kinds of problems. But at this news she lost her composure and ran out of the office like a lunatic.

She could have imagined anything else, but not this. She had been a faithful, honest wife and had dedicated her life as a lawyer to helping people. Why had this disaster happened to her? She ran until she reached the ocean.

When she was a girl, she loved walking on the beach, barefoot, feeling the tickle of the sand under her feet. Now, it offered her no comfort.

"It can't be!" she screamed.

She didn't want to cry, but her heart was a volcano waiting to explode, her mind an endless whirlwind, and the tears rolled down her cheeks.

"It can't be!" she screamed again.

The waves washed her screams into the depths of the sea. The seagulls seemed like buzzards waiting to devour her corpse. That was what she felt like—a corpse.

She walked. She cried. She screamed. She felt like a dead woman. Her husband had killed her.

A morbid idea rolled around in her head. If she threw herself from a cliff, she could end the drama she was living. She was condemned to die anyway.

She brushed the thought away, and her mind traveled into the past. She remembered standing on the balcony of her home and vivaciously calling down to the young man below,

> Get away from my window, crazy little boy!
> My mother doesn't like you, and neither do I!

—words from a poem she had learned as a child.
Ricky had responded with lines from the same poem:

> Tomorrow morning you'll wake up crying for the one
>   who was never your husband or boyfriend or lover.
> But he loved you best, and that is enough!

Their courtship was stormy. Her parents never accepted Ricky, and they had all the reasons in the world for opposing her relationship with him. The long-haired young man with tattoos on his arms had no ambitions, and he was wasting his youth in bars.

But Ricky's persistence finally won out. No one was able to dissuade Lucía from marrying him. She went ahead despite the advice and warnings of her parents, other relatives, and friends.

The first weeks of their marriage were wonderful, but the honeymoon soon ended. When the young couple returned to the realities of daily life, their eyes began to open to the vast differences between them. Lucía was growing professionally as a lawyer in a powerful international law firm. Ricky had no goals. He hid his failures behind the word *destiny* and spent long hours in bars, offering the excuse that he was looking for work. He never contributed financially to their support and drank liquor too freely. Lucía sensed that he was also using drugs.

Most women would have had more than enough reasons to end the meaningless relationship. Not Lucía, though. She had deep religious convictions and believed that marriage is a life-long commitment. She was willing to bear the consequences of her mistake till the last of her days.

*   *   *   *   *

As Lucía sat on the rock, listening to the roar of the waves and remembering the details of her life with Ricky, her heart filled with rage. What he had done to her wasn't fair. If he wanted to live recklessly and was willing to die because of the choices he made, that was his business—let him suffer the consequences. But he had no right to infect her. Staring at the sea, she began to cry again.

Several hours later, Lucía went home. She entered the house determined to end the sick relationship that had resulted in her infection.

Ricky was sitting in the living room, waiting for her to arrive. When she came in, he saw the fire in her eyes. It scared him. He had never before seen that look on her face.

Ricky had known for a month that he was sick. That was why he insisted that Lucía go to the doctor. Her late return told him that she had learned she was infected too.

He threw himself at her feet. "Forgive me, dear," he cried. "I've destroyed your life."

That was the last straw. Did Ricky think that if he just asked for forgiveness, everything would get better? Lucía was overcome by disgust and hate. They had a terrible argument. The more he cried and begged for forgiveness, the more she hated him. She yelled terrible words at him—as if through her words she could expel the cursed virus that coursed through her veins.

Suddenly, she lost all connection with reality. She ran to their bedroom, grabbed the pistol she kept in a drawer, and shot Ricky six times. Then she left to wander through the darkness of the night.

At dawn, she was sitting on the rock beside the sea once more. That was where the police arrested her.

*   *   *   *   *

The following months were painful. Lucía's broken health was only one of the many problems that arose like impassable mountains before her. The judicial process she went through drained her emotionally. She had terrible nightmares. And the weight of the guilt she bore was crushing. Consequently, she had no strength to fight off the opportunistic diseases that attacked her beleaguered immune system.

It was under these circumstances that God's Word reached out and touched Lucía. Her first contact with the Bible occurred while she was in prison. Very early one morning the radio in her cell carried the broadcast of an evangelist preaching about Mary Magdalene.

When Mary Magdalene had been caught in adultery, "religious" men dragged her out to be stoned for her sin. From a human point of view there was no escape. Everything was lost. But humanity's greatest need is God's greatest opportunity. With a few scribbled words Jesus drove her accusers away.

Then He looked at her with love and said that He didn't condemn her. " 'Go,' " He said, " 'and sin no more' " (John 8:11).

The words touched Lucía's numb feelings. The next day she acquired a Bible and began reading. And when she was released from prison on bail, she continued reading the sacred Book.

One day Lucía met Ricardo. He knew the scriptures well, and he offered to teach her about them. Then, as the days passed, the woman condemned to death by a terrible disease discovered extraordinary truths.

June was approaching, and Lucía's trial would begin soon. The district attorney had declared that he planned to ask for the maximum sentence. Her defense lawyer tried to allay her fears. He said, "The judge will take into account the fact that you committed the crime in a state of deep emotional disturbance." Still, her anxiety grew with every passing moment. The future seemed hopeless. Even if the trial went well, her days were numbered: science offered no cure for her ailment.

* * * * *

One evening as Lucía studied the Bible with Ricardo, the subject of the judgment she would be facing in a few days came up. "Did you know that the Bible talks about a judgment too?" Ricardo asked.

"Yes," Lucía answered. "I know that we will all face the final judgment, and it scares me because of what I did."

"You don't have to be afraid," Ricardo comforted. "Jesus is willing to be your Defense Attorney, and He has never lost a case. But I'm not talking about the final judgment that will take place when Jesus comes back. That will really be just the execution of the sentence pronounced on the guilty. All the righteous will receive eternal life, and all who have rejected Jesus will die.

But before the execution of the penalty, there has to be an investigative judgment during which all the cases are analyzed one by one."

"Does that mean there will be a judgment before Jesus comes?"

"Yes, it does. The Bible says, 'We must all appear before the judgment seat of Christ, that each one may receive the things done in the body, according to what he has done, whether good or bad' " (2 Corinthians 5:10).

"I think that if our eternal fate is at stake, we should know when that judgment takes place," Lucía said.

"God has revealed the date, although not everybody knows about it," Ricardo replied. "It's in the Bible, but only those who study with humility can understand it."

"Will you explain it to me?"

"Of course. I'll begin with something the apostle John wrote in the last book of the Bible: 'I saw another angel fly in the midst of heaven, having the everlasting gospel to preach to those who dwell on the earth—to every nation, tribe, tongue, and people—saying with a loud voice, "Fear God and give glory to Him, for the hour of His judgment has come" ' " (Revelation 14:6, 7).

"The hour of His judgment *has come*?"

"Yes, it has come."

"Does that mean the judgment is happening at this very moment?"

"Exactly."

"How do you know?"

"Let's take a look. The verse I just read is in Revelation, the last book of the Bible. To understand Revelation, we must view it in the light of the Old Testament. And in order to know when the judgment started, we need to study the history of Israel—God's people in the Old Testament."

"Was Israel judged on some special day?" Lucía asked.

"Israel had a holy day called the Day of Atonement. Jews still celebrate it. They call it *Yom Kippur*. The literal meaning of that name is 'day of covering.' The word *covering* carries the connotation of forgiveness, of pardon.

"On the Day of Atonement, the Israelites were supposed to renew their commitment to God and confirm their repentance so they could be forgiven and cleansed. ' "On that day the priest shall make atonement for you, to cleanse you, that you may be clean from all your sins before the LORD" ' [Leviticus 16:30]. On that day the chief priest sacrificed animals and purified the sanctuary.

"Now note this verse from the New Testament: 'It was necessary that the copies of things in the heavens should be purified with these [the blood of animals], but the heavenly things themselves with better sacrifices than these. For Christ has not entered the holy places made with hands, which are copies of the true, but into heaven itself, now to appear in the presence of God for us' [Hebrews 9:23, 24].

"If you look closely at this passage, you will conclude that there is a sanctuary in heaven. Israel's sanctuary on earth was just a copy of the heavenly sanctuary."

"That's surprising. I never would have imagined a sanctuary in heaven." Lucía was intrigued.

"A lot of people find it surprising, but the Bible is clear: there is a sanctuary in heaven. Now consider this, Lucía: if the day of purification for Israel's sanctuary was a day of judgment for the Israelites, then it would make sense that the day of purification for the heavenly sanctuary would be a day of judgment for all humanity."

"Does the Bible mention such a day of purification for the heavenly sanctuary?"

"Yes, it does," Ricardo replied. "And, of course, the date when that purification begins in heaven is the date when the judgment begins here on earth."

"Where is the date? Show me—I want to see." Lucía was curious.

Ricardo opened the book of the prophet Daniel and read verse fourteen of chapter eight: " 'He said unto me, Unto two thousand and three hundred days; then shall the sanctuary be cleansed' " (KJV).

"Wait a minute!" Lucía exclaimed. "How do you know that verse is talking about the heavenly sanctuary?"

"It's simple. Israel's sanctuary was purified every year. But this verse pictures a single purification. Note this also in Hebrews: 'Christ has not entered the holy places made with hands, which are copies of the true, but into heaven itself, now to appear in the presence of God for us; not that He should offer Himself often, as the high priest enters the Most Holy Place every year with blood of another—He then would have had to suffer often since the foundation of the world; but now, once at the end of the ages, He has appeared to put away sin by the sacrifice of Himself' " (Hebrews 9:24–26).

"OK," Lucía agreed. "I can see that it is talking about a single purification and undoubtedly refers to the sanctuary in heaven."

"Let's go back to the prophecy in Daniel. It says that after twenty-three hundred days the sanctuary will be cleansed. If we discover the end point of that prophecy, we'll know when the heavenly sanctuary was purified—in other words, on what day the judgment of the human race began."

"This is fascinating!" Lucía exclaimed, and then she asked, "Can you tell me more about this prophecy?"

"Numbers chapter fourteen, verse thirty-four and Ezekiel chapter four, verses four through six indicate that in symbolic

Bible prophecies, a day represents a literal year," Ricardo said. "In other words, the twenty-three-hundred-day period specified in this prophecy points to twenty-three hunded literal years.

"In order to know when this period ends, we need to know when it started. The prophecy came to Daniel with the following warning:

"The vision of the evenings and mornings
Which was told is true;
Therefore seal up the vision,
For it refers to many days in the future" [Daniel
   8:26].

"Daniel wrote that when he received the vision and the warning, he 'fainted and was sick for days; . . . [He] was astonished at the vision, but no one understood it' [verse 27].

"The next chapter of Daniel's book pictures the prophet pleading with God about matters related to the prophecy of chapter eight. Daniel says that as a result, the angel Gabriel came to him again and told him, ' "At the beginning of your supplications the command went out, and I have come to tell you, for you are greatly beloved; therefore consider the matter, and understand the vision:

"Seventy weeks are determined
For your people and your holy city, . . .
To make an end of sins,
To make reconciliation for iniquity,
To bring in everlasting righteousness. . . .

"Know therefore and understand,
That from the going forth of the command

To restore and build Jerusalem
Until Messiah the Prince,
There shall be seven weeks and sixty-two weeks. . . .

"He shall confirm a covenant with many for one week;
But in the middle of the week
He shall bring an end to sacrifice and offering"
(Daniel 9:23–25, 27).

"Ricardo," Lucía complained, "to be honest with you, I'm not understanding a thing you're saying."

"Don't worry, I'll explain it," Ricardo replied. "The verses I just read contain all the information we need to understand the prophecy.

"There are four basic points. First, according to what we just read, the prophetic period of twenty-three hundred years began when the order went out to 'restore and build Jerusalem.' History records that King Artaxerxes of Persia gave this order in the year 457 B.C. That is when the prophetic period began.

"Second, the prophecy says that from 457 B.C. 'until Messiah the Prince' would be 'seven weeks and sixty-two weeks.' This totals sixty-nine prophetic weeks—or, in other words, four hundred eighty-three literal years. The word *Messiah* literally means 'Anointed One,' and Jesus was anointed by the Holy Spirit at His baptism. If we start in 457 B.C. and count four hundred eighty-three years, we come to the year A.D. 27—the very year when, according to history, Jesus was baptized. [See Luke 3:1–3, 21, 22.] Can you see how precisely the prophecy was being fulfilled?"

"Yes, it's amazing. Please go on," Lucía responded.

"OK, let's go on to the next point—number three: The

prophecy mentions one more week, or, in other words, seven more years, which takes us from A.D. 27 to A.D. 34—the year the Jews stoned Stephen and the Christians began preaching the gospel to the Gentiles in earnest. At that time, the probationary period assigned to the Jewish nation came to an end. 'Seventy weeks are determined for your people' the angel said when explaining the prophecy to Daniel."

"That's amazing too!" Lucía said.

Ricardo smiled and said, "There's more. Point number four: The prophecy stated that in the middle of the last week—in other words, in A.D. 31—'He shall bring an end to sacrifice and offering.' This part of the prophecy was fulfilled when Jesus was crucified. With His death, the animal sacrifices that Israel made were no longer necessary. And history indicates that Jesus actually did die in the middle of that final period of seven years."

Lucía commented, "Once more, the prophecy was fulfilled!"

"That's right. Up through this point, everything was fulfilled precisely as it was prophesied. What is fascinating is that Daniel was given this prophecy nearly six hundred years before Christ's birth, yet it all came to pass."

"Well, what about the twenty-three hundred years? Where do they come in? When are they fulfilled?"

"Stay with me. If we extend the rest of the twenty-three hundred years beyond the four hundred eighty-three years, then we must conclude that this prophetic period ended in A.D. 1844. That means that according to the prophecy, the purification of the heavenly sanctuary was to begin in 1844. So the great judgment of the human race also was to begin in that year."

"That is surprising—and sobering. People should know about such an important event!" Lucía exclaimed.

"That's right," Ricardo replied. "We're not talking about something still to come. According to Bible prophecy, the process of determining human destiny has been going on since 1844!"

"Is that why the three angels appear in Revelation and declare, 'the hour of His judgment has come'?"

"Exactly. Notice that the angel is flying, which implies speed. That means the message is urgent—there's no time to lose. Notice also that the message is declared in a loud voice. It can't be ignored any longer. It must be announced to the whole world, to benefit all people."

"You know, Ricardo," Lucía said, "I always thought the judgment had to do with the plagues and catastrophes that are to occur before Jesus' second coming."

"A lot of people think the same thing," Ricardo answered. "The Bible does speak of a time of plagues. But they are the result of the judgment—part of the sentence, the penalty. They're not the judgment itself. The judgment is the process in which the cases are reviewed. The process involves a judge, a lawyer, a prosecutor, witnesses, and evidence. Notice how Daniel describes the heavenly scene:

> "I watched till thrones were put in place,
> And the Ancient of Days was seated;
> His garment was white as snow,
> And the hair of His head was like pure wool. . . .
> A fiery stream issued
> And came forth from before Him.
> A thousand thousands ministered to Him;
> Ten thousand times ten thousand stood before Him.
> The court was seated,
> And the books were opened" (Daniel 7:9, 10).

At this point in the conversation, many emotions tugged at Lucía's heart: sadness, happiness, surprise, fascination, wonder, and a slight bit of fear that clouded the joy of her discovery. She and Ricardo had spent nearly two hours studying the prophecies about the judgment. During all that time, immersed in the wonderful Bible truths she was learning, she had completely forgotten the drama she was living. She was facing a judgment on this earth and would have to give an account before a human court for the crime she had committed.

Ricardo noticed the sadness that hung over her like a cloud. "Look at this promise," he said. " 'My little children, these things I write to you, so that you may not sin. And if anyone sins, we have an Advocate with the Father, Jesus Christ the righteous' " (1 John 2:1).

"Thank you, Ricardo," Lucía stammered, trying to hide a tear.

"Lucía," Ricardo said, "Jesus is your Advocate. Do you believe that? Do you want to entrust Him with your case? With God, everything is already settled. You don't have to fear human beings. If Jesus is at your side, even if you go through the water, you won't get wet."

That afternoon both of them knelt in prayer. While Ricardo was praying, Lucía felt as though an invisible hand touched her head and a fire burned in her bones. Afterward, a feeling of peace and forgiveness washed over her.

*   *   *   *   *

At Lucía's first trial, she was sentenced to several years in prison. Her lawyer appealed to the Supreme Court, and while she waited for that trial, she was freed. She never went to court again. Instead, she went to the hospital, the victim of a common cold that brought the dreadful complication of pneumonia.

Friends and family came to bring her encouragement, but such peace flooded her heart that she encouraged them instead.

"What has happened to you?" a friend asked upon finding her so unexpectedly optimistic.

"I have met Jesus," Lucía said, and she smiled as she spoke.

As the days passed, Lucía's life slowly waned. She had loved the wrong man, and as a result of her faulty decisions, a grotesque crime was written on the next-to-last page of her life story. What is more important, though, is that Lucía filled the last page with repentance, confession, and forgiveness.

Before losing consciousness, Lucía told her pastor, "I see God sitting on His throne. White-robed angels are serving Him. The book is open, and Jesus is writing with His blood: 'Lucía, My dear daughter: ACQUITTED.' "

* * * * *

I am dreaming. In my dream, I walk the streets of the New Jerusalem. I am dazzled, excited. My heart overflows with gratitude to God. I don't deserve anything; I am there only by His grace. I will never have enough words to express to my Jesus all the love and gratitude I feel.

Suddenly, a woman approaches dressed in a white robe and wearing a crown of victory on her head. Her eyes shine with the brilliance of redemption. She hugs me and says, "Thank you for telling me about Jesus that morning on the radio in my prison cell."

I don't know her. I've never seen her before. She introduces herself. She is one more victory for God's love. She is Lucía.

Chapter Ten

A Defeated Enemy

A shriek knifed through the jungle, jolting the whole village awake. In the silence that followed, all that could be heard was the buzzing of insects, like a rumor of tragedy. Curious people peered from their huts and asked, "What was *that*?" As if in answer, they again heard the hair-raising, heartrending cry. This time they ran to the place where the screams came from.

On the ground beside an old log, Alfredo was writhing as though possessed by a thousand demons. His face was contorted, his eyes were bulging, and he was biting his lips so hard that they bled. At first glance, he appeared to be having an epileptic fit.

He wasn't.

The problem had started a while ago. Alfredo and his wife had the worst argument they'd ever had. They'd started arguing the day she began attending meetings where people studied the Bible.

Alfredo was the village witch doctor. He was a man who made every effort to preserve the traditions of his tribe. He got drunk on *masato*.* He chewed on coca leaves when he went on long hunting forays into the jungle—he loved hunting—and during the mysterious rites he practiced.

The members of his tribe were superstitious. They venerated the stars, birds, shadows, and anything that was frightening. Their worship included horrifying, bloody rites that Alfredo led. No one's life was sacrosanct. Those whom his accusing finger identified as guilty would die, victims of the savagery of their own tribe. The attackers knew that tomorrow they might find themselves in the same situation, but they could do nothing to avoid the tragedy. They all feared Alfredo.

No! Alfredo had decided. He wouldn't allow his wife to continue attending the meetings. The people who studied the Bible were strange. They didn't drink the *masato* or chew coca leaves or participate in the village religious ceremonies. How could they live like that? Alfredo didn't believe in the Bible, and he knew that if his wife kept studying it, he'd face big problems.

Years before, many people from his tribe had been converted to the gospel by a gringo who came from North America. But Alfredo's father had never believed in such things, and Alfredo had inherited his skepticism. He didn't know about God's ability to transform lives. He had never imagined the wonders God works in order to impress hard hearts.

One splendid, sunny day, Alfredo sat cross-legged on a rock, resting and gazing at the majestic scenery before him. He saw the intense green of the river and the trees, the clear blue of the sky, and the white of a few scattered clouds. Butterflies and flowers added accents of color to the natural tableau.

Though Alfredo had seen this picture many times before, he still gazed at it with the special feelings of someone who loves

---

*An alcoholic beverage made from fermented cassava.

his surroundings. A torrent of emotions overpowered his soul. *Beloved jungle! Beloved sky! Beloved river!* he thought.

But he didn't love everything.

Cursed Protestants!

A series of family fights paraded through his mind. That very morning he had beaten his wife because he had seen a Bible in her hands.

"Cursed Protestants!" This time he spat out the words, his face red with rage as he rolled a cigarette.

He lit the cigarette and smoked in silence. The jungle seemed unchangeable under the scalding sun, which itself traveled unchanging over the valley. Only human beings changed.

His wife was changing. She had changed a lot lately.

"Cursed Protestants!" It was all their fault. His heart was full of animosity. For years he had been the most feared and respected man in the whole village. Now he was losing his authority. Why did those people have to come and bring their Bibles?

The sun was still high in the sky. Occasionally, small motorized launches filled with passengers disturbed the calm water of the river. Suddenly, loud bangs and thumps and despairing cries surprised Alfredo. One of the launches had hit a rock and was sinking fast.

The people who knew how to swim made their way toward the riverbank. Some of the women and children, who apparently didn't know how to swim, were struggling desperately to survive. Several of the villagers were attempting to rescue them.

As Alfredo watched the drama playing out in front of him, he saw a black object floating in the water. He thought he might be seeing the back of somebody's head. He threw himself into the water and with firm strokes pushed himself quickly through the water until he reached the object. He was surprised to see that it was a book. He grasped the book and swam back to the bank.

When Alfredo emerged from the river, he realized he had rescued a Bible—the very Book he so despised. He stood frozen in place, wondering what to do. All the other solid objects in the boat had sunk. Only the Bible had floated. How could a book float?

That night Alfredo went out of his house and looked up at the sky. A cool breeze caressed his face, and he breathed deeply. Never before had the night seemed so beautiful. The buzzing of the insects in the jungle around him comprised background music for his thoughts. The events of that afternoon had disturbed him greatly. His eyes were drawn to the Bible he had rescued. Why hadn't it sunk? Was God trying to tell him something?

Alfredo was superstitious. He feared the unknown—things he couldn't understand. So now he was upset. There was something mysterious about this Book. What it was he could find out only by reading it. But his pride rose up like a wall before him. To read the Bible would be to admit that he was wrong and his wife was right. No. He could never do that. He hated everyone who read the Bible.

There are a lot of people like Alfredo. They hear God's voice calling at the door of their heart, but they harden themselves out of pride and prejudice. Still, God calls them. He says,

> "I have loved you with an everlasting love;
> Therefore with lovingkindness I have drawn you"
> (Jeremiah 31:3).

Divine Mercy was patient with Alfredo. He was a man in conflict. All his life he had served his gods sincerely, but then he came face to face with the Bible. He began to read it. And in it he discovered the only true God, Creator of heaven and earth. When Alfredo began to see how small his gods were beside the Creator of the universe, his mind became a whirlpool of frustrations.

The Bible says,

> The heavens declare the glory of God;
> And the firmament shows His handiwork (Psalm
>   19:1).

> Lift up your eyes on high,
> And see who has created these things,
> Who brings out their host by number;
> He calls them all by name,
> By the greatness of His might
> And the strength of His power;
> Not one is missing (Isaiah 40:26).

How could he look at the splendid sky of the jungle and deny the existence of a God who had created all the things he considered gods—the rain, the sun, the stars? It wasn't easy to accept a sovereign God and to renounce everything he had believed all his life. When he read the Bible, all his beliefs came crashing down around him.

He began to have terrible nightmares. They reached their climax that night when the villagers heard him scream. Unseen hands had pulled him out of his hut and left him lying where the villagers found him. Then he perceived a horrifying reality: He had never served any gods after all. He'd never been useful to anyone. He'd merely been the unwitting slave of *Camari*—the devil!

Alfredo heard the devil's laughter that night. He saw gleaming eyes glare at him from the darkness, and the sound of flapping bat wings nearly scared him to death.

Alfredo was no coward. He had never been afraid of darkness or the night. But now he felt alone, terribly alone, and he began to feel like he was suffocating. He knew he had gone too far. *Camari* wasn't willing to let him go.

The apostle Paul declared, "We do not wrestle against flesh and blood, but against principalities, against powers, against the rulers of the darkness of this age, against spiritual hosts of wickedness in the heavenly places" (Ephesians 6:12).

There are "rulers of darkness" who are willing to destroy people's lives if they decide to follow Jesus. These demons do so in many ways. Sometimes they take complete possession of fragile people such as Alfredo. Other times they take advantage of habits and vices in order to enslave those who want to run to Jesus. When these strategies don't work, they even provoke persecution. They'll use any and every method available in their efforts to keep people away from God. That's why the apostle Peter advised, "Be sober, be vigilant; because your adversary the devil walks about like a roaring lion, seeking whom he may devour" (1 Peter 5:8).

If you've heard about God's Word but walk blindly on, then the enemy has no reason to bother you. Without Christ, you are going down the road to eternal death anyway. But the day you decide to follow Jesus, you will discover that all of Satan's rage is directed right at you. That is why Peter advised us to "be vigilant." Paul added, "Be strong in the Lord and in the power of His might. Put on the whole armor of God, that you may be able to stand against the wiles of the devil" (Ephesians 6: 10, 11).

Putting on God's armor takes time. No one can get dressed

in an instant. When Paul advised us to put on the whole armor of God, he was referring to spending time with God in daily Bible study and prayer. If you take the time to do that—if you dress yourself in the divine armor—the enemy's strategies for destroying your life will fail, and he'll have to go away.

*　*　*　*　*

The enemy fought many battles against Jesus, but he lost them all. The first battle took place in heaven. John described it: "War broke out in heaven: Michael and his angels fought against the dragon; and the dragon and his angels fought, but they did not prevail, nor was a place found for them in heaven any longer. So the great dragon was cast out, that serpent of old, called the Devil and Satan, who deceives the whole world; he was cast to the earth, and his angels were cast out with him" (Revelation 12:7–9).

This text tells us that the enemy lost that first battle. He was thrown out of heaven to this earth, where he has dedicated himself to capturing the allegiance of the human race. The principal weapons he uses are deceit and seduction. Truth terrifies him. But when Jesus came to this world, He said, " 'I am the way, the truth, and the life' " (John 14:6).

The devil's expulsion from heaven didn't stop him. He didn't give up. When Jesus was born of the virgin Mary, He was God incarnated in the form of a baby. When the enemy saw the fragileness of that tiny newborn, he tried again to defeat Jesus. He took over Herod's heart and led him to order the killing of all the infants in Bethlehem. But the angel of the Lord came to Joseph in the middle of the night and told him, " 'Arise, take the young Child and His mother, flee to Egypt, and stay there until I bring you word; for Herod will seek the young Child to destroy Him' " (Matthew 2:13). So Jesus was safe. Once more Satan was defeated, and his malevolent intentions failed.

But the enemy didn't give up. He attacked a third time. This time he found Jesus in the desert, weakened by forty days of fasting. He thought this would be his great opportunity. Rather than attempting to attack Jesus directly on this occasion, he used the weapon of temptation. However, once more he was defeated and Jesus was victorious.

But the enemy still didn't give up. He attacked again. This time he entered the hearts of the political and religious authorities of that age, and they condemned Jesus. Now there appeared to be no way to escape. Jesus would certainly die.

And Jesus actually did die on the cross of Calvary that Friday afternoon. Then Satan thought he had achieved his goal. He thought that Jesus was finally defeated. When Jesus' body was placed in a cold tomb, the entire universe heard Satan's gloating laugh of victory. The shadow of death enshrouded the world, and it appeared that all was lost.

But on the third day, the tomb was opened and death gave way to life! Jesus broke the power of the lord of darkness, and his sinister smile disappeared.

Since that time the devil has had no more right to destroy lives. He has finally and definitively been defeated. Jesus has won decisively. Now, He gives His victory to every person who believes in Him.

* * * * *

That night in the Peruvian jungle the villagers knelt around Alfredo's shaking form. It was a terrifying spectacle. He screamed heartrendingly. The believers prayed, claiming the victory that Christ won on the cross and that His resurrection confirmed.

The enemy trembled and then threw the witch doctor's body against a tree, and Alfredo roared like an injured beast. However, the roar didn't actually come from Alfredo. Rather, it was from the enemy. He knew his control over Alfredo was ending.

The believers continued singing and praying. It was a critical moment. They felt like they were fighting the battle of the ages—a crucial battle in the war between good and evil.

Alfredo wanted to be free from the supernatural power that had dominated him all his life. Barely conscious, he called out the name of Jesus. The enemy gave a final, hair-raising shriek and departed, and Alfredo fell to the ground exhausted. Then, though Alfredo was trembling and in a cold sweat, he knelt and, raising his eyes to heaven, thanked Jesus for His liberating power.

The Christian's hope for victory over the forces of evil is not mere wishful thinking or utopian dreaming. It is certain. Every time the enemy encounters Jesus, he is defeated. That is why James told us, "Submit to God. Resist the devil and he will flee from you" (James 4:7).

The enemy tempts us. That is what he most enjoys doing. But though he uses all his weapons and strategies, he can't defeat us without our permission. If we don't agree to his seductions, he has to retreat and take all his temptations with him.

Today, the devil is a defeated enemy. There's no reason for us to be bested by him. So, take hold of Jesus' victory by faith. Decide not to be afraid. Don't hesitate to leave the darkness and enter the marvelous light of Christ. Don't allow false ideas, traditions, and habits to overpower the Holy Spirit's call.

Today is the day. Now is the time. The Lord Jesus Christ is standing before you with His arms open wide, willing to receive you and make you new.

If Alfredo hadn't called out to Jesus that dark night, he would probably have died in Satan's grasp, condemned to eternal death. He believed, he accepted, and he was saved.

You too can experience the salvation Christ offers.

*   *   *   *   *

Though the sun was nearing the horizon, it was still terribly hot in the jungle. I had been walking for nearly five hours, and I was tired, thirsty, and hungry, but I continued to move forward, cutting a path with a machete.

When I reached the village, the people ran to welcome me. After all the greetings, they took me to the hut where I would be staying for the next few days.

At suppertime, Raquel, the wife of my host, served delicious fish soup and roasted cassava root. I sat at the table, eager to begin eating. In front of me, my host took his place. He was very old, with long, white hair. His face was marked by scars—remains of the traditions of his former life.

"Will you please pray, pastor?" he asked calmly.

I watched him in admiration. I already knew his story. He was a living example of the liberating power of Christ. He was Alfredo.

The Invitation is also available in Spanish!
2008 Spanish Sharing Book
Invitación
Alejandro Bullón
ISBN: 0-8163-9348-6

If you found the stories in this book inspiring, you will appreciate this story of redemption also.

Life Without Parole
Rick Fleck

"I first became conscious of the pain and then of the stench of rotten meals and an unflushed toilet. *Where am I?* I blinked, terrified, seeing only four cement walls. Memories of the past night caught up with me as I groaned in anguish. I was busted."

Nothing in Rick Fleck's childhood had suggested that he would end up in prison for life on a murder charge. Rick was a third-generation Adventist. He grew up living close to nature on a farm near Canadian Union College. His parents sacrificed to send him to Christian schools. He was outgoing, popular, and a star athlete.

Fleck gives an honest account of himself as a college dropout obsessed with money, prestige, and life in the fast lane. At first cocaine was just something to take so he could work harder and earn more money. But then . . .

ISBN 13: 978-0-8163-2228-2
ISBN 10: 0-8163-2228-7

Three ways to order:
1. Local Adventist Book Center®
2. Call 1-800-765-6955
3. Shop AdventistBookCenter.com